The
Phoenix
Affirmations

The Phoenix Affirmations

A NEW VISION
for the FUTURE *of*
CHRISTIANITY

✝

ERIC ELNES

JOSSEY-BASS
A Wiley Imprint
www.josseybass.com

Copyright © 2006 by Eric Elnes. All rights reserved.

Published by Jossey-Bass
A Wiley Imprint
989 Market Street, San Francisco, CA 94103-1741   www.josseybass.com

No part of this publication may be reproduced, stored in a retrieval system, or transmitted in any form or by any means, electronic, mechanical, photocopying, recording, scanning, or otherwise, except as permitted under Section 107 or 108 of the 1976 United States Copyright Act, without either the prior written permission of the Publisher, or authorization through payment of the appropriate per-copy fee to the Copyright Clearance Center, Inc., 222 Rosewood Drive, Danvers, MA 01923, 978-750-8600, fax 978-750-4470, or on the web at www.copyright.com. Requests to the Publisher for permission should be addressed to the Permissions Department, John Wiley & Sons, Inc., 111 River Street, Hoboken, NJ 07030, 201-748-6011, fax 201-748-6008, e-mail: permcoordinator@wiley.com.

Unless otherwise noted, Scripture quotations are from New Revised Standard Version Bible, copyright © 1989, Division of Christian Education of the National Council of the Churches of Christ in the United States of America. Used by permission. All rights reserved.

Scripture quotations marked "The Message" are from *The Message* by Eugene H. Peterson, copyright © 1993, 1994, 1995, 1996, 2000, 2001, 2002. Used by permission of NavPress Publishing Group. All rights reserved.

Jossey-Bass books and products are available through most bookstores. To contact Jossey-Bass directly call our Customer Care Department within the U.S. at 800-956-7739, outside the U.S. at 317-572-3986, or fax 317-572-4002. Jossey-Bass also publishes its books in a variety of electronic formats. Some content that appears in print may not be available in electronic books.

Library of Congress Cataloging-in-Publication Data
Elnes, Eric.
  The phoenix affirmations : a new vision for the future of Christianity /
Eric Elnes.— 1st ed.
     p. cm.
  Includes bibliographical references and index.
  ISBN-13: 978-0-7879-8578-3 (pbk.)
  ISBN-10: 0-7879-8578-3 (pbk.)
  1. Christianity—Forecasting. I. Title.
  BR121.3.E46 2006
  269—dc22   2005037205

FIRST EDITION
PB Printing 10 9 8 7 6 5

CONTENTS

This book is dedicated to

God

The spiritually homeless of the world who yearn
for the face of Christianity to resemble
more closely the face of Jesus.

The many who volunteer time and talent to
CrossWalk America—an organization tirelessly
and joyfully working to create a home
for the spiritually homeless.

Melanie, Arianna,
and Maren

# THE AUTHOR

Eric Elnes is a biblical scholar with a Ph.D. from Princeton Theological Seminary. He is also senior pastor of Scottsdale Congregational United Church of Christ in Scottsdale, Arizona (www.artinworship.com), known internationally for its innovative, multisensory worship experience called The Studio. Dr. Elnes serves as co-president of CrossWalk America (www.CrossWalkAmerica.org), an organization committed to resourcing, strengthening, and celebrating the emerging progressive Christian faith. He also serves on the faculty of the Center for Arts, Religion and Education, in Berkeley, California.

Dr. Elnes authored the original version of the Phoenix Affirmations and served as lead editor of its subsequent revisions. He is also the author of *Igniting Worship: The Seven Deadly Sins* (Abingdon, 2004) and is the original developer of "The World's Most Dangerous Bible Study"—an approach to studying Scripture in conversation with popular music and film used around the world and published in numerous issues of Princeton Theological Seminary's audio journal, *Cloud of Witnesses*.

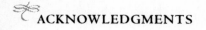

ACKNOWLEDGMENTS

This book is the product not only of scholarly research and pastoral reflection but of many public and private conversations for which I am most grateful. Many of these conversations have been with members and friends of Scottsdale Congregational United Church of Christ in Scottsdale, Arizona—a congregation I have served as senior pastor for ten years. I have especially benefited from conversations with Associate Pastor Rev. Katharine Harts, and with those who have attended Worship Team meetings, Bible study groups, and our Theology on Tap sessions. Over the course of a year, our conversations regarding the *Phoenix Affirmations*—which frequently lasted for hours— brought us several steps closer to the core of our passion and faith, and closer to each other as well.

Other lively and helpful conversations have been held while planning a walk across America to raise awareness of the *Phoenix Affirmations* with CrossWalk America (http://www. CrossWalkAmerica.org). CrossWalk America is a unique, nonprofit organization at the center of the emerging movement within Christianity. I am especially indebted to conversations with copresident, Rebecca Glenn, as well as board members Ray Steiner, Scott Logan, Brad Wishon, Brenda Stiers, Mac Schafer, Fletch Wideman, and Tom Jelinek.

Still other conversations contributing directly to this book were held with the clergy of No Longer Silent: Clergy for

Justice, in Phoenix, Arizona, who served as the initial incubator group for the Phoenix Affirmations. Their passion for justice, tolerance, and equality for all people has been an inspiration for many years. Also important have been the clergy and scholars associated with the Center of Theological Inquiry in Princeton, New Jersey—particularly those with the Western Regional Pastor-Theologian program who helped greatly in bringing the Phoenix Affirmations into their present form.

Finally, conversations with my wife, Melanie, and daughters, Arianna and Maren, as well as my good friend and mentor Bruce Van Blair, have contributed significantly to this work. I love you more than words can say. And with respect to the words I *can* say, they are all said much better thanks to the extraordinary insights of my editor at Jossey-Bass, Sheryl Fullerton.

It should be obvious that "my" thoughts and insights—at least the good ones—are actually connected to a vast web of relationships. These relationships have been, and still are, united by a single purpose and passion: changing the face of Christianity as we know it to more closely resemble that of Jesus.

—E.E.

INTRODUCTION

"I'm tired of being a Christian butt," Jenny exclaimed with obvious exasperation.

I thought this was rather unusual language coming from a high school choral director and member of my congregation in Scottsdale, Arizona. It's not her choice of words but the sentiment that surprised me. In the past few years, I have only seen Jenny get more excited about her faith, not less.

When Jenny first cautiously started coming to my church, she had not actively participated in a church for over twenty years. She considered herself "spiritual but not religious."

"I have a problem with organized religion," she had told the friend who originally invited her.

"Not to worry," her friend said. "My church is more like *disorganized* religion. We've got kids running around all over the place; visual artists, dancers, jazz and classical musicians weaving in and out of worship, and it seems like we've got small groups exploring every subject you can imagine, from hiking to social justice to independent films. My favorite is a Bible study that meets in a brew pub."

This last one intrigued Jenny. Instead of showing up at church the next Sunday as her friend suggested, she joined us at the brew pub. Jenny will tell you that the kind of faith she encountered from participants at the brew pub marked the beginning of her personal "Great Awakening" about Christianity.

Since that day, she has been like the Energizer Bunny of spiritual exploration and discipleship. She has rarely been immersed in less than three or four small groups. She has helped with our teen mentoring program and assisted in our outreach to homeless families. Jenny almost never misses a Sunday worship experience and sometimes helps lead it.

So you can imagine my surprise when Jenny used *Christian* as a modifier for *butt*. "What do you mean by that?" I asked.

"I mean," she replied without hesitation, "I'm tired of having always to qualify the word *Christian* when I tell people I'm going to church. I might as well say I'm radioactive. They get a surprised look on their face and say, "Not *you*, Jenny. You don't seem like the Christian type." So I find myself throwing in more and more *but*s all the time: 'I'm a Christian, but . . . but . . . but . . .'"

"Oh, I get it," I responded. "I thought you meant 'Christian butt'—b-u-t-t."

She went right on, "Why should I have to explain to people, 'I'm a Christian, but I don't think homosexuals are evil. . . . I'm a Christian, but I believe women are equal to men . . . but I'm concerned about poverty . . . but I care about the earth . . . but I don't think people who believe differently from me will fry in hell for eternity . . .'?"

Why is it that the word *Christian*, which should stand for people of extravagant grace and generosity, who are abundantly loving, who are associated with acts of courage, justice, and compassion, has become synonymous with *butthead*?

Consider the kinds of voices that have claimed to speak for Christianity in the media in the past few years. In the following three examples, can you identify the speaker?

Example 1: The dust had hardly settled after the collapse of the Twin Towers in New York City on September 11, 2001, when news of a gay chaplain who died heroically while attending to the wounded and of a gay man who had led an attempt to overthrow the terrorists on Flight 93, was drowned out by this proclamation: "I really believe that the pagans, and the abortionists, and the feminists, and the gays and lesbians who are actively trying to make that an alternative lifestyle . . . I point the finger in their face and say, 'You helped this happen.'" Who is this leader? *Hint:* For many years, he was the head of the so-called Moral Majority and has also said, "The ACLU is to Christians what the American Nazi Party is to Jews."

Example 2: The *Washington Post* reported this statement from a prominent Christian leader: "[The] feminist agenda is not about equal rights for women. It is about a socialist, anti-family political movement that encourages women to leave their husbands, kill their children, practice witchcraft, destroy capitalism and become lesbians." This same leader is no less charitable toward fellow Christians who are not of his exact fold, exclaiming, "You say you're supposed to be nice to the Episcopalians and the Presbyterians and the Methodists and this, that, and the other thing. Nonsense. I don't have to be nice to the spirit of the Antichrist." Who said these things? *Hint:* This leader has also advocated that the U.S. government assassinate the democratically elected president of Venezuela.

Example 3: In an internationally televised worship service in which this minister warned his congregation about homosexuals seeking marriage rights, he made the following statement: "I'm gonna be blunt and plain: If one ever looks at me like that [with amorous intent], I'm gonna kill him and tell God he died." Amazingly, his congregation reacted neither with shocked silence nor with gasps of disapproval but with laughter and applause. Who is this leader? *Hint:* Several years ago, he appeared on national television weeping, asking God and the rest of us to forgive him for cavorting with prostitutes.

As you may have known, these statements come from Jerry Falwell, Pat Robertson, and Jimmy Swaggart, respectively. All three are popular "go to" figures when the media want to hear "the Christian position" on various issues. These leaders are not alone. Indeed, a great number of Christians with similar views are presently cued up behind them striving to be the next spokespeople for Christianity in the American mass media.

With so much focus in the media on the religious extremists, it is easy to get the impression that Christians don't have much to do with Jesus anymore. Worse, in the absence of a strong, positive, clearly articulated Christian alternative, more and more people start believing that Jesus might actually agree with the extremists and want nothing to do with people who think like that.

Consider the following factors, which may surprise you: studies consistently show that nearly nine out of every ten people in America identify themselves as Christian. Yet only four in ten will tell you they've been to church lately. If you scratch below the surface of these four, you'll find that only two or three actually have been to church. Of these two or three, many have significant reservations about being there.

A *Newsweek*/Beliefnet poll conducted in 2005 is illustrative of this collective unease within American Christendom."[1] When asked if a person from another faith can be saved or go to heaven, a full eight of every ten Christians answer yes. Particularly surprising is the fact that seven in every ten Christian Evangelicals say yes, and nine in every ten Catholics. Considering that a major tenet of faith in both the Evangelical and Catholic communities is that there is no salvation outside the Christian faith (and some will argue that there is no salvation outside their particular "brand" of Christian faith), these figures are downright stunning.

What do they tell us? Clearly, there is a very strong sense of spiritual homelessness in America today. When seven or eight of every ten American Christians either are frustrated with their church or have dropped out of church participation entirely (mostly the latter), it takes no great leap of the imagination to affirm that the majority of Americans are feeling profoundly disconnected from their faith community.[2] Because these Americans are usually silent, they are also invisible. It is relatively easy for churches and especially Christian leaders to bury their heads in the sand and pretend that there is no crisis. However, if, as Christian mystic and theologian Teilhard de Chardin suggests, we are not human beings having a spiritual experience in life but spiritual beings having a human experience,[3] then the level of spiritual disconnectedness indicates a crisis of immense proportions. More people suffer from spiritual homelessness than suffer directly from terrorism, economic downturns, or even physical homelessness. This is not in any way to deny or diminish the seriousness of these other threats. It is simply to acknowledge that the problem of spiritual homelessness has been grossly underrated. Indeed, it could be argued that our lack of spiritual connection to each other has diminished our ability to deal constructively with these other threats.

There is reason to hope, however. This book is about hope, if nothing else. If you are a "Christian but . . . ," you are far from alone. In fact, you may very well be connected in important ways to the majority of Christians in our country who, whether they realize it or not, are part of a fundamental shift taking place in the nature of Christianity. This shift has been at work for more than a century. As Marcus Borg has observed, the shift is largely a product of Christianity's encounter with the modern and postmodern world, including science, historical scholarship, religious pluralism, and cultural diversity.[4] Aside from flare-ups here and there, such as when Princeton Theological Seminary split into two different seminaries in the late 1920s over strife related to the shift, it has until recently been a relatively quiet one in the public sphere. As a whole, most Americans did not begin to recognize a shift had even begun until the fruits of it started spilling out of the seminaries and into the public. Now this movement is generally referred to by scholars and church leaders as a shift toward "progressive Christianity" or an "emerging Christian faith." It may very well turn out to be the most important shift in Christianity in the past five hundred years or more.

This book may be considered a snapshot taken at the heart of this shift. To be sure, the photo is of a moving target. However, it is an important picture in that it specifies and reveals the disparate and sometimes invisible developments that are taking place underneath the surface of Christianity. More important for you, this snapshot may even afford a glimpse of what is going on at the heart of your own spiritual development, giving rise to the joys and anxieties you experience on a day-to-day level, whether you are Christian or not.

In the following pages, we will explore a set of twelve principles known as the Phoenix Affirmations. The Phoenix Affirmations were originally penned by a group of clergy and laypeople from Phoenix, Arizona, in an attempt to articulate clearly the broad strokes of the emerging Christian faith.[5] Word spread, and soon pastors, theologians, and biblical scholars from every mainline denomination, with degrees from seminaries and divinity schools such as Harvard, Princeton, Yale, Andover-Newton, Claremont School of Theology, Pacific School of Religion, Luther Seminary, and Saint Paul School of Theology added input. They were joined by laypeople and progressive Christian leaders from around the country.

In other words, the Phoenix Affirmations are not the product of some obscure religious faction trying to make a name for itself. They are mainstream Christian leaders' best take on where the emerging Christian faith stands today and where it may be headed in the future.

If the people responsible for the Phoenix Affirmations and others have correctly identified this shift, there is much reason for hope for the spiritually homeless in America. The Phoenix Affirmations depict a far more tolerant, joyful, and compassionate face of Christianity than the media typically portray. They reflect commitments to environmental stewardship, social justice, and artistic expression as well as openness to other faiths. They uplift often overlooked values such as the need for recreation and play, prayer and reflection, and the right to be responsible for decisions governing one's body. And they are biblically based, even in their assertion that the Bible should be taken seriously and authoritatively but not literally.

Most important, they are steeped deeply in the words of Jesus, who said that the two greatest commandments in all of life are to love God with heart, mind, soul, and strength and to love one's neighbor as oneself.[6] Accordingly, the Affirmations take on a threefold structure, based on the Three Great Loves identified by Jesus and affirmed within Judaism: Love of God, Love of Neighbor, and Love of Self. Ultimately, it is these Three Great Loves that define best what the emerging Christian faith is all about. It is a faith that invites all people to a great and wondrous party—a joyful and daring celebration where the only ones not included are those who turn down the invitation.

It almost goes without saying that the Phoenix Affirmations are not meant to be a static set of principles to stand for all time. If the authors do not believe the Scriptures are without error, how could they assert otherwise for the Affirmations? In fact, to make this point perfectly clear, they attached a version number to them—currently 3.8—indicating that the Affirmations are the product of continual modification and will certainly be amended in the future in light of new awareness and deeper understanding of what is believed to be God's call. You may or may not resonate with each and every word or principle. That's OK! The Affirmations are also not meant to serve as some form of test of faith against which a person's Christian commitments are to be verified. They serve only as a snapshot of an exciting moment in Christian history and perhaps an equally exciting moment in the development of your own spiritual awareness. If you at least resonate with the spirit of the Affirmations, chances are you will find them helpful to your path in some way.

My congregation has been studying the Affirmations intensively for nearly a year, devoting three worship services to each Affirmation as well as making them the focus of adult and children's programming. We have taken them home for private study and reflection and shared them with interested friends around the country. The effect of our focus on the Phoenix Affirmations has been nothing short of magical. This is not to claim that the Affirmations themselves are magical or carry any mystical quality. Rather, our personal and communal engagement with them has led to no small amount of transformation. People keep telling me how helpful it is to finally have a set of principles that positively and joyfully proclaim what they have always believed but have never been able to articulate clearly. The Affirmations help make faith more concrete, providing a sense of direction, interconnectedness, and forward motion to the faith journey. In this sense, they make the faith more livable.

My congregation's experience is not in any way unique. As the Affirmations have spread, the authors are continually hearing from study groups, progressive Christian organizations, and individuals—Christians, non-Christians, and even people of no faith at all—that the Affirmations speak to them deeply.

One woman from Seattle, having studied the Phoenix Affirmations on a spiritual retreat, choked up and said, "Now *this* is the kind of faith I want to hand down to my children!" Another man from Phoenix who grew up Catholic and left any form of church long ago told me, "These Affirmations represent a movement I've always wanted to be a part of but never knew existed."

Each of the following chapters focuses on one of the twelve Affirmations. You will find a summary cited first (one sentence per Affirmation), followed by the full version (three paragraphs per Affirmation). This will be followed by my reflections on the Affirmations, based on personal engagement with them as well as input gleaned from laypeople in my church. I have also benefited greatly from input by the leadership of an organization called CrossWalk America (http://www.CrossWalkAmerica.org), a progressive Christian group that will be carrying the Phoenix Affirmations across the country starting Easter Sunday, April 16, 2006, in a 2,500-mile walk ending in Washington, D.C. There the Affirmations will be symbolically "nailed to the door of America." Simultaneously, they will be nailed to the headquarters of every major Christian denomination in the country.

Finally, I will give practical suggestions for integrating each principle into your everyday life. It is hoped that individuals, communities of faith, and ecumenical organizations will take these suggestions as the first step in drawing up their own set of implications particular to their setting. Thus, for instance, you may wish to create the [Your Name] Implications. A church might create the First Presbyterian Church Implications. An ecumenical group might organize its activities around the Cleveland Implications. The implications are limited only by your creativity.

A deep and exciting shift is taking place within the Christian faith. It started before you were born and will continue long after you leave the earth. You are in the middle of it. None of us can claim to know exactly where it's going or where it will end up (at least not for a few centuries). However, if present developments are any indication, it will emerge as a faith that is far more buoyant, expansive, and compassionate than anything we have imagined in the last half millennium, if not longer. Use this book to orient you to the emerging faith in its current form, and if you choose, jump in and emerge with it! There is room enough for everyone.

AFFIRMATION

one

**Walking fully in the Path of Jesus without
denying the legitimacy of other paths
that God may provide for humanity**

AS CHRISTIANS, WE FIND spiritual awakening, challenge, growth, and fulfillment in Christ's birth, life, death, and resurrection. While we have accepted the Path of Jesus as *our* path, we do not deny the legitimacy of other paths God may provide humanity. Where possible, we seek lively dialogue with those of other faiths for mutual benefit and fellowship.

WE AFFIRM that the Path of Jesus is found wherever love of God, neighbor, and self are practiced together. Whether or not the path bears the name of Jesus, such paths bear the identity of Christ.

WE CONFESS that we have stepped away from Christ's Path whenever we have failed to practice love of God, neighbor, and self or have claimed Christianity is the *only* way, even as we claim it to be *our* way.

Whoever is not against us is for us.
—JESUS (MARK 9:40)

Don is a Christian conservative who showed up at my office one day wanting to discuss his daughter Carrie's salvation. On her eighteenth birthday, Carrie up and announced she had converted to Buddhism. Needless to say, this had a rather chilling effect on the celebration. The whole family, including grandparents, aunts, and uncles, was thrown into a panic. After numerous attempts to convince Carrie to return to the Christian faith, each of which led to a greater rift between them, Don decided to seek the advice of the senior pastor of his Bible church. After listening to all the ways in which the family had attempted to lead Carrie back to the fold, the pastor advised Don and his family to disown their daughter.

"You can't allow Carrie to have an influence on your other children," he said. Don had two other children—a fifteen-year-old boy and a twelve-year-old girl. "They're younger than Carrie," the pastor reminded. "A bad apple can spoil the whole barrel if you're not careful. How would you feel if one or both of your remaining children were to suffer in hell as a result of Carrie's mistakes? You need to cut her loose. Besides, showing Carrie tough love like this might just create a big enough crack in Carrie's heart to allow Jesus to slip back in."

Don didn't know what to do. His fatherly compassion for Carrie made him want to keep her close and show her love and acceptance no matter what her beliefs. Yet compassion for his other two children made him want to do as the pastor advised. His conflicting sense of compassion was tearing him apart!

A year earlier, Don had heard, from a friend who attends my church, that we had spent eight weeks exploring the relationship between Jesus' Sermon on the Mount and certain Zen Buddhist stories (*koans*). Back then, he had been put off by our openness to other faiths. Now he was curious.

"Your church seems to have a different attitude toward the other religions," he told me in a challenging tone. "I'd like to hear your justification for it." Then, lowering his eyes and voice slightly, he continued, "Right now, I've got a very personal reason for hearing you out. Do you believe that all religions are just as legitimate as Christianity?"

After asking a few questions to assess where he was coming from, I answered, "As a Christian, I've always been an appreciator of the major religions of the world. I draw insight from them and sometimes learn more about my own religion through studying what others believe. However, since I've never been a practitioner of any of these other religions, I'm in no better position to judge the legitimacy of, say, Buddhism than a Buddhist would be to assess the legitimacy of Christianity. What I can tell you is that there is a strong and coherent strand in both the Christian and Jewish faiths that acknowledges that God has created other legitimate paths that we have no business condemning."

"But didn't Jesus say something about him being 'the way, the truth, and the life' and that 'no one comes to the Father except through me'?" Don countered.

"Yes, he says that in John 14:6," I said.

"Then how can you say that there may be other paths?"

"First, you have to understand the context in which Jesus is speaking. He's having a conversation with *his disciples*. He's not talking to Buddhists or Taoists or Zoroastrians. He's saying that *his disciples* find God through him. There is no compelling reason to believe that Jesus is making a blanket statement about all the followers of all the other religions."

"But how can you be so sure that people of other faiths can be saved?"

"I believe this because Jesus himself says so," I responded.

"What?" John exclaimed in disbelief. "I've never heard anything of the sort."

I took a Bible off the shelf, and we explored Scripture together. We had a lengthy conversation that afternoon about heaven, hell, and salvation, some of which I'll relate under Affirmation 9. Mostly we explored what Jesus had to say that might have some bearing on other religions.

One of the passages Don found most suggestive is John 10:4–16, where Jesus says, "I am the good shepherd. I know my own and my own know me, just as the Father knows me and I know the Father. And I lay down my life for the sheep. *I have other sheep that do not belong to this fold.* I must bring them also, and they will listen to my voice. So there will be one flock, one shepherd."

Some believe that Jesus is calling here for the conversion of those of other faiths to Christianity. Yet Jesus refers to adherents of other faiths ("other sheep that do not belong to this fold") who *already* belong to him ("I have . . ."), who *already* know him ("I know my own and my own know me"), and therefore can be expected to respond to him when he calls, as sheep respond to the familiar voice of their shepherd ("they will listen to my voice"). Jesus is not calling for sheep of different folds to change shepherds. Jesus is simply asking his disciples to recognize that the God they know in Christ is also the God of others. Ultimately, the human family is one flock, with one shepherd.

It is important to understand what Jesus is *not* saying here as well as what he *is* saying. What he's decidedly not saying is, "Different strokes for different folks." Nor is he saying, "Anyone can worship the god of one's choice, and it's all good, no matter whom or what one worships." Rather, Jesus is asserting that a number of faiths ultimately worship the same God. Which faiths? They aren't identified. We may surmise, however, that faiths that truly follow the "one shepherd" actively promote the love of God, neighbor, and self, as Jesus did. Jesus does not seem to think people walking in the path he reveals should be spending all their time worrying about which other paths are watched over by the same shepherd and which are not. He demonstrates much more enthusiasm throughout the Gospels for his disciples to concentrate on walking their own path and offering hospitality to those they meet along the way.

In 2004, I took a pastoral sabbatical sponsored by the Lilly Endowment, traveling to two places—India and Ethiopia—where Christianity has been around since ancient times but has grown up outside the limelight of Western Christianity. Few Westerners realize that Christianity in India goes back at least to the second century and perhaps all the way to the apostle Thomas, who Indians claim made his way to southern India and started seven churches before being martyred in Chennai (Madras) in the late fifties of the first century. My object in India was to study Christian worship and spiritual practices, looking for what is distinctive about them and what commonalities are shared with Western Christians. I was also very interested to observe how Christianity related with the other religions of India.

One of the most fascinating stops in my journey was at a Christian ashram (learning community) called Shantivanam about a hundred miles inland from Chennai in southeastern India. The ashram, which houses a couple of dozen Benedictine monks and nuns, was once the home of Father Bede Griffiths, a Benedictine whose life project was studying the relationship between Christianity and the religions of India, particularly Hinduism and Buddhism. Shantivanam is a beautiful place in which residents practice a very simple lifestyle of prayer and worship, study and manual labor, and service to the community. There are few luxuries at Shantivanam — especially luxuries that Westerners have grown to believe are necessities, such as air conditioners on hot summer days, washers and dryers, and sit-down toilets. Simple vegetarian meals are consumed as a community in silence so as to maintain an attitude of "mindfulness" about the bounty placed before each person.

One of the highly distinctive aspects of Shantivanam is the commitment to integrating Christian faith with Indian culture in a way that preserves the integrity of both. Monks and nuns dress in Indian attire, iconography depicts Christian saints dressed in Indian garb, and worship . . . ah, worship! Worship is joyfully and unapologetically Christian (sound familiar?) yet integrates complementary insights and aesthetic forms from Hindu worship.

The spiritual director of Shantivanam, Father John Martin, is one of those people who just seem to radiate holiness. Father Martin is in his mid to late forties. His short black hair, toned muscles from manual labor, and warm, cinnamon-bark complexion make him a strikingly handsome leader. He is also strikingly humble, with a confident though welcoming demeanor, a quick smile, and eyes that burn bright with warmth and passion when he speaks.

My family and I spent several days at Shantivanam worshiping, studying, and speaking with the community. On the last full day of our sojourn, I sat down with Father Martin in a small building reserved for prayer, meditation, and instruction, and we talked about the relationship between the world religions.

Father Martin asserts that the major world religions can be likened to hikers climbing up different sides of a mountain. Each tradition has discovered a unique route for reaching the top. While they are climbing the mountain, the traditions cannot necessarily see one another. Individuals within the climbing parties may not even be aware that others are ascending the mountain. They think they alone are making the ascent. Yet when they reach the top, the climbers are surprised to find one another. Each party has reached the same goal by a different route.

I find Father Martin's characterization of the relationship between the faiths helpful for a number of reasons. First, it provides a concrete way of understanding and articulating how different faiths may ultimately lead to the same place. Second, the analogy helps us understand that God may allow for different paths, each with its own integrity. A Hindu may find a way to the top through withdrawal from the world, while a Christian may find it through immersion in the world on behalf of justice. Sometimes Christian liberals are overly quick to claim the unity between the world religions and get rather sloppy about it. They say things like "They're all just saying the same things. They're really no different." Well, they really *are* different. Their routes up the mountain engage different terrain, with different obstacles and challenges, different vistas, and different places of rest. On the other hand, sometimes Christian conservatives take the differences between the faiths to be signs that all religions but Christianity are following the wrong path. The mountain analogy helps us see how differences between faiths may be celebrated instead of either minimized (by liberals) or condemned (by conservatives). It also illustrates the fact that God's plan for the world is larger than our human minds can comprehend. Despite significant differences of approach to God, and regardless of where, to whom, or when we happen to be born, we are all included in God's love, which exceeds our wildest imagination.

What I especially like about Father Martin's characterization is that it sheds light on what Jesus was saying when he spoke of the sheep who are not of the same fold but who have the same shepherd. Jesus does not simply say "all paths are legitimate" or "anything goes." Rather, he calls from the mountaintop to his sheep, who are making their way up the paths provided for them. He encourages us all as we traverse obstacle and vista alike, assuring us that other flocks are on their way up as well, on other sides of the mountain. When we finally reach the top, we can expect to live not only with the Good Shepherd but with the whole human family as one flock.

Affirmation 1 stands solidly within this theological worldview. While it acknowledges that Christians walk a path God has created up the mountain and further claims an awareness that God may provide other paths leading to the summit, it does not go so far as to claim to know with absolute certainty which paths are authentic and which are rabbit trails. How could we? It would be like a climber on one side of the mountain trying to speak with authority about paths on another side of the mountain that the climber has never been on. The climber may read about these paths in books. The climber may even have spoken with people on another side of the mountain. All this may lead the climber to believe that the paths seem to be heading to the same place. But any serious climber knows that only those who have climbed the path can speak with authority about where it leads and how it gets there.

In this respect, Affirmation 1 no more claims "different strokes for different folks" than Jesus does. It does not say "all paths are legitimate." Rather it simply acknowledges that Jesus, as the first one to climb our particular path to the top, assures us there are other ways up the mountain.

WALKING THE TALK

The first and perhaps most important implication of Affirmation 1 is for the Dons of the world, who worry about the fate of those they love who may be or become practitioners of other faiths. For some, the Christian path is not the one they are best suited to climb. It may be necessary to explore other paths until one is found that fits and elevates the soul. Often if Christians do not get overly distraught about the fact that someone they love has "left the fold" and they continue to offer authentic love and acceptance of that person, the person ultimately decides that the path he or she was on before wasn't so bad after all and gladly returns. And if not, then the person may very well be led by God to a more suitable path. The point is that our relationship with God is at the center of the quest, not simply our relationship with a particular path.

Second, it is unfortunate and naive for a practitioner of any faith to claim that theirs is the only "true" path. However, it is perfectly appropriate for a person of a particular faith to claim that hers is the "best" path. So long as that claim is made on the individual level, one would hope that all travelers who are making their way up the mountain have searched around enough to be convinced that they have found the best path for them. A person should feel neither ashamed about this belief nor angered to hear that others feel that their path is better *for them*. It is far more rewarding and also more faithful to swap stories from the journey with earnestness and conviction. If the people of other faiths with whom we are in dialogue decide to convert to our faith as a result of this sharing, fine. However, conversion is not the ultimate purpose of interfaith dialogue. Sharing the joy and wisdom gleaned from our climbing experience is.

Third, particularly when we are in conflict with other countries whose dominant faiths may be different from our own, it is also critically important to examine our underlying assumptions about their religions. In wartime, each side endeavors to dehumanize the enemy so that citizens will more readily support the war effort. Often religion gets drawn into the dehumanization process (it is both easy and effective). When this happens, the consequences generally outlast the immediate conflict.

Whether or not one believes that going to war in Iraq was a good idea, for instance, it may be reasonably argued that our willingness to allow religion to be used in the dehumanization process in other conflicts, such as the Israeli-Palestinian situation, made us much more willing to go to war than would have been the case otherwise. As persons of faith, we should actively resist forces that use religion for the purposes of dehumanizing the enemy lest we throw obstacles in paths God has created for humanity's good and lest we throw an obstacle in our own path by failing to properly show the love and respect for God and God's people that Jesus himself commands.

two

Listening for God's Word, which comes through daily prayer and meditation, studying the ancient testimonies which we call Scripture, and attending to God's present activity in the world

AS CHRISTIANS, WE LISTEN for God's Word in the living presence of the Holy Spirit, praying every day, and discerning God's present activity in our world. We also study and revere the ancient records that we call Scripture, recognizing that they were formed in distinct historical and cultural contexts yet were informed by God's Spirit, which transcends all ages and times. Most of all, we seek the meaning of salvation, of Jesus' life, death, and resurrection as presented in Scripture and discerned in daily life.

WE AFFIRM that the Path of Jesus is found where Christ's followers engage in daily prayer and meditation, as well as personal and community study and interpretation of Scripture, as central ways God's continuing voice is discerned in everyday life.

WE CONFESS that we have moved away from Christ's Path when we have claimed that God's Word is restricted to what may be contained in a written document or that either the recording of God's Word in Scripture or our interpretation of it is infallible. Further, we have moved away from the Path when we have allowed the mere fact of Scripture's fallibility, or our own, to dissuade us from seeking God's Word in Scripture, prayer, and reflection on daily life.

Every happening, great and small, is a parable whereby
God speaks to us, and the art of life is to get the message.
— **Malcolm Muggeridge**

In my sophomore year in high school, I had the unhappy experience of watching my minister be asked to resign because the congregation decided that the church "had no life in it." Several members thought that if we could find a minister with a strong knowledge of and respect for the Bible, our church would become vital again.

The minister they called—the Reverend Bruce Van Blair—was, and is to this day, the wisest, most earnest, and most devoted student of the Scriptures I've ever met. Bruce brought with him a breathtaking knowledge of ancient history that made the Bible come alive. He would preach and teach about Abraham and Sarah, King David, or Jesus and his disciples, and you would swear he'd just been with them yesterday. You wanted to know more about their stories and their understandings of life and spirituality because they seemed to understand it a lot better than anyone in our day. Our sleepy little church began to come back to life!

One day, however, about six months into his ministry, Bruce called the congregation together for a special meeting. Bruce wanted to tell us something about the Bible—namely, how to interpret it properly.

Bruce acknowledged that there were a number of biblical stories the congregation—and many other Christians, including himself—dearly loved. Then he cited examples where biblical claims clearly contradicted reliable historical records or where they even contradicted claims made elsewhere in the Bible.

The congregation was shocked; some parishioners were squirming in their seats. Then Bruce said that no matter how many people swear that every line of Scripture is without error, this kind of certainty often comes more from a *lack* of appreciation for Scripture than from true love and respect for it. He insisted that our love for the biblical stories—even the ones he had just shown us were historically inaccurate—would actually become more dear, that they could be considered "true" even if they never happened. He said that the ancients were not particularly concerned with factual history as we understand it today. Whereas we tend to look for the who, what, when, and where when we read history, he said, the ancients were far more concerned with the why. Once we begin reading the Bible like the ancients did, that's when it comes to life, making you want to dive right in and swim in its deep waters.

Some people in the congregation—especially those who had been most insistent that we hire a Bible-loving pastor—left murmuring darkly about the future of Bruce's ministry on Mercer Island. I, however, felt an unusual "lightness of being" during the meeting even though I was scared out of my wits about the potential implications. My more conservative friends at school claimed that if you question even one fact in the Bible, you'll soon question another and then another until finally the bottom will fall out and you'll throw the whole thing away as irrelevant.

I visited Bruce in his office not long after the meeting to talk to him about all the questions I had about the Bible. Nearly thirty years later, our discussion is still burned in my mind.

When I told Bruce my concern that a fundamental teaching of Christianity was that Scripture is without error, he challenged me by asking whether the fundamental teachings of Christianity are those that have something to do with Jesus. He asked me if Jesus taught that the Bible is without error. I told him that I assumed he did, but Bruce pointed out that Jesus doesn't say that anywhere. In fact, Jesus held the opposite view. Jesus' Bible was the Old Testament. He obviously read it thoroughly and took what he read seriously, but he did not read it literally. Bruce used the Sermon on the Mount in Matthew 5 as an example. Here Jesus directly challenges the biblical tradition, saying, "It was said to you by the men of old . . . but I say to you . . ." Those "men of old" were the writers of Scripture. Throughout the Sermon on the Mount, Jesus is challenging the Bible of his day, claiming a higher awareness and truth than it was proclaiming. Clearly, nobody had yet invented all the doctrines and creeds—Christianity had not yet become a social structure designed to control people and their thinking. Early Christians didn't even have written scriptures for the first three centuries.

Bruce explained that Jesus came to show us a better way. Part of that better way is questioning what has come before and moving to higher ground. Jesus didn't say that only he could do that. He wanted us to do it too. Bruce then took out a Bible, marking two places and handing it open to the first one to me.

I read from Genesis 17:14: "Any uncircumcised male who is not circumcised in the flesh of his foreskin shall be cut off from his people; he has broken my covenant."

Then I turned the book to his next marker, Galatians 5:1–6: "For freedom Christ has set us free. Stand firm, therefore, and do not submit again to a yoke of slavery."

Bruce stopped me at this point, noting that the "yoke of slavery" to which Paul was referring is the burden of holding on to claims made in the Bible that God is trying to move us beyond. The passage continues: "Listen! I, Paul, am telling you that if you let yourselves be circumcised, Christ will be of no benefit to you. Once again I testify to every man who lets himself be circumcised that he is obliged to obey the entire law. You who want to be justified by the law have cut yourselves off from Christ; you have fallen away from grace."

"In other words," Bruce said to me, "you have to choose who you love more: the Bible or Jesus. Paul didn't consider even the most respected and widely practiced laws in the Bible to be infallible, like circumcision. You have to remember that Paul had at one point been a biblical literalist. Before his conversion, he traveled the countryside persecuting people for not following what was commanded in Scripture. At one point, Paul had such reverence for Scripture that he even had people killed for not living according its laws. After his conversion, Paul still respected and loved Scripture yet felt that following Jesus set him free from bondage to what had come before."

The early church fathers argued, often with great heat, over which writings should be included in the Bible and which should not. They challenged them openly and often had long lists of reasons why they approved or disapproved. They never claimed that the truth of their Bible was self-evident. They themselves could never even agree on which writings should be included.

The canon of Scripture—the body of texts the church as a whole counts as authoritative—was never created by unanimous vote. The New Testament canon is set by human usage, not by divine decree. Bruce then told me how Protestant reformer Martin Luther felt about the Epistle of James—which Luther called the "epistle of straw"—and how he ignored the Book of Revelation. Luther, in fact, vocally contradicted any writing that he felt did not keep Christ's Gospel of grace and love central and paramount.

It has only been in the last couple of hundred years that this whole notion of biblical inerrancy arose. It was biblically ignorant, literalistic, self-appointed leaders who championed the new doctrine. The doctrine seems to have addressed people's longing for (false) security and certainty even as it gave Christian leaders more leverage and control over their congregations and created a rat's nest of scriptural contradictions that would all have to be explained away in order to maintain the doctrine.

Jesus said, "He who believes in me will also do the works that I do; and greater works than these will he do, because I go to the Father." Doesn't a true father want his children to be better and to achieve more than he did? Of course, in what area and in what manner depend on which father.

Bruce told me that if we do not find and live by a greater faith than our fathers did, we're doomed. Jesus said, "Unless your righteousness exceeds that of the scribes and Pharisees, you will never enter the kingdom of heaven" (Matthew 5:20). The scribes and Pharisees were the religious fundamentalists of Jesus' day. If we do not find and live by a better faith than our fathers had, we are doomed to a life here as limited, cut back, and watered down as they had.

Over the next fifteen years of Bruce's ministry on Mercer Island, I watched the little church grow in numbers and spirit. The life that congregation shared together was anything but limited, cut back, and watered down. At times it seemed like everyone in the congregation was involved in a Bible study and had attended a prayer retreat or two in the past year. Bruce proved that to question faith is not to disown it but to claim it with deeper passion, joy, and conviction.

From the day I left Bruce's office, I have never wished I had held on to my uneasy belief in the inerrancy of Scripture. I have grown to love Scripture too much to do so.

When I went to seminary, I found, much to my surprise, that biblical literalists aren't nearly as literal as they claim to be. No matter how loudly one claims to live by the plain, simple, infallible words of the Bible, in reality, everyone has a "canon within a canon." That is, everyone holds certain aspects of Scripture to be more authoritative than others. If you have any doubts, just ask a literalist, "Which of the following do you believe in?"

- Publicly stoning to death a rebellious son or daughter
- Wearing clothes made with only one kind of fiber or eating foods made with only one kind of grain
- Men having multiple wives
- The keeping of slaves
- Short people, thin people, people with hunched backs, and people with impaired eyesight being banned from serving as clergy

These are only a small sampling of the codes of behavior advocated in the Old and New Testaments that almost everyone excludes from the body of passages considered to be authoritative.

What I found in seminary is that Christians throughout the centuries have used certain principles for discerning the authoritative from the nonauthoritative in Scripture. One particularly trustworthy principle for interpreting Scripture is called the Rule of Love.

The Rule of Love

The Rule of Love goes back at least as far as the fourth century and probably before then. It is essentially this: if a passage in Scripture appears to contradict the essence of Jesus' command to love God with all our heart, mind, soul, and strength or to love our neighbor as ourselves, then the passage, or our interpretation of it, must be held suspect.

Before the so-called doctrine of inerrancy was popularized two centuries ago, the Rule of Love served the Christian community as the most consistently used principle by which one could discern an appropriate "canon within the canon." The doctrine of inerrancy undermined this principle. Pastors convinced their congregations that all of Scripture is equally inspired and without error. Thus passages that in past eras had been set aside or at least debated rigorously on the grounds that they failed to measure up to Christ's commands about love were now given full legitimacy. A command to publicly stone a rebellious child theoretically carries as much weight as the command to love one's enemies and do good to those who hate you.[1]

The emerging Christian faith is as much about stepping back as stepping forward when it comes to biblical interpretation. It steps forward in its embrace of modern scholarship and its commitment to hearing God's new Word revealed in the ancient texts. Yet it is also about stepping back to a way of viewing Scripture that is not as concerned with historical accuracy as it is with its truth-bearing quality and that measures those truths against the standard of how well they reflect Jesus' command to love God, neighbor, and self.

Prayer and God's Activity

"To clasp the hands in prayer," Karl Barth is said to have observed, "is the beginning of an uprising against the disorder of the world."

Prayer outranks Scripture in the hierarchy of things spiritual. No matter how highly one values Scripture, it is no substitute for direct contact with God. A book—even an inspired book like the Bible—does not outrank a relationship. The Bible is an incredible compendium of *other people's* relationships with God that were recorded to help us know how to seek *our own relationship* with God. Our spiritual ancestors would have thought us to be not very interested in spiritual life if they heard us claim that one could have a relationship with God primarily through a book.

In the early centuries, a period that almost everyone agrees was a high-water mark in Christian history, no one read the New Testament. Not only did it not yet exist, but few people would have been able to read it because they were for the most part illiterate and books were in any case far too expensive for the common person to own. Books were all hand-copied until the invention of the printing press in the 1400s. Even then, Martin Luther observed that the Bible is a "closed book" unless it is read in conjunction with prayer.

Looking through the Gospels, we find that prayer was Jesus' own primary spiritual practice. A brief glance through the Gospel of Luke, for instance, makes this clear:

> But now more than ever the word about Jesus spread abroad; many crowds would gather to hear him and to be cured of their diseases. But he would withdraw to deserted places and pray. (Luke 5:15–16)

> Now during those days [Jesus] went out to the mountain to pray; and he spent the night in prayer to God. (Luke 6:12)

> Jesus was praying alone, with only the disciples near him. (Luke 11:1)

[Jesus] was praying in a certain place, and after he had finished, one of his disciples said to him, "Lord, teach us to pray, as John taught his disciples." (Luke 18:1)

If someone like Jesus needed to spend so much time in prayer to discern God's will, does it not stand to reason that prayer should be a significant part of our daily lives?

Surveys consistently find that more than nine out of ten of us pray regularly. Some studies even suggest that more people pray than believe in God! Likely you pray, but maybe you are a bit uncomfortable with prayer. How long do your prayers generally last? One or two minutes? Three to five minutes? If so, I have bad news and good news for you. The bad news is that you are not likely to ever have a very interesting prayer life with this much time devoted to connecting with God. Certainly there are very short prayers that can change our lives forever. However, as a basis for a true, ongoing relationship with God, there's just too much static coming over the "God channel" to be cleared in five minutes. As the Buddhists say, there are too many monkeys shaking the trees.

The good news is that if you've only been taking about five minutes, your satisfaction as a person of prayer will *dramatically* increase if you practice some basic principles that are hard at first but become much easier with experience. It takes a while to get there, but you can get there. What once seemed so utterly unreasonable to do becomes not only reasonable but utterly unreasonable to do without.

The observation is this: *you need to spend thirty minutes each day in prayer.*

That's right, thirty minutes. But not thirty minutes like the five you're now spending in prayer. In order to pray for a full half hour, you need to set aside certain false assumptions that I call the "sacred cows of prayer."

When it comes to the following three sacred cows, I think the saying "Sacred cows make the best hamburger" aptly applies. Grind them up. Form them into a patty. Fry them, add lettuce, tomato, and a couple of buns, and be done with them.

Sacred Cow 1: "I truly don't have time."

Martin Luther is said to have observed, "As it is the business of tailors to make clothes and of cobblers to mend shoes, so it is the business of Christians to pray." For the Christian, prayer—and skillful prayer at that—is not optional.

When you're doing something you love, how fast does a half hour go? Really fast, for most people. Prayer can be so engaging that it passes that quickly. You can find thirty minutes no matter how busy you are, *provided you feel the time you've invested is worth it.* There will always be days when prayer feels more like a chore—like nothing "happened." But these will be more than offset by times when something grabs you completely by surprise; when awareness dawns that had eluded you before; when you feel like you're connected to a Presence that is thoroughly aware of you and actually cares about you deeply. This may happen during the actual time you're praying or come later on as a result of having increased your sensitivity to "overhearing" God during your prayer time.

In seminary, I had a theology professor who was a pretty average lecturer three out of every four class sessions. But about once a week, he'd say something that would completely rock my world. I'd think about what he said not only after class but for weeks, months, and in some cases years afterward. I quickly found myself quite forgiving of days when I learned nothing particularly interesting because I knew I could count on him to deliver a steady share of zingers as well. That's how prayer works. It may not necessarily be interesting every day, but it is interesting often enough that I've been willing to show up for a half hour or more each day for the last twenty-five years.

Sacred Cow 2: "I'm not good or religious enough."

In all my years as a minister, I've found this sacred cow in the background of most problems people bring to me. When it comes down to it, most of us do not feel good or religious enough to deserve much of God's attention. We may even hope God hasn't noticed us lest God be disappointed in us.

Yet God is not in the morals business. God is in the relationship business. And since we humans are the ones God has chosen to be in relationship with, this means that God is also in the forgiveness business, the mercy business, the business of love and compassion. God does not count our sins before agreeing to meet with us. Likely you are more interested in your sins than God is.

Abraham Lincoln once recollected, "I have been driven many times upon my knees by the overwhelming conviction that I had nowhere else to go. My own wisdom and that of all about me seemed insufficient for the day."[2] Imagine if Lincoln had put off praying until he could better impress God with his wisdom. As Lincoln apparently knew very well, we pray to God because we *need* to pray. We can and should pray *before* we feel like we know what we're doing, *before* we feel we deserve God's love and acceptance, *before* we get over being angry or afraid.

Sacred Cow 3: "I must have something to say."

One of the greatest misconceptions about prayer is that you must have something to say—a list of things to ask for, a list of things to give thanks for, and perhaps also a list of wise and pious observations about life. In other words, prayer is mostly about talking to God.

The exact opposite is true. Prayer is far less about talking than listening. There is an apocryphal story about an interview with Mother Teresa. In response to a remark that she prays every day, a reporter asks her, "What do you say to God?"

"I don't say anything," Mother Teresa responds. "I listen."

"Then what does God say to you?"

"God doesn't say anything," she replies. "God listens."

Confused, the reporter asks, "How can you pray when both you and God do nothing but listen?"

"Explaining this," Mother Teresa responds, "would take far longer than you have time for."

As this story suggests, the basic stance in prayer is that of deep listening, and there may not be a lot of action on God's part that is immediately perceptible. The experience may be more like the sound of falling snow. You do not hear directly the sound of falling snow. What you hear, if you're paying attention, is the change of acoustics in your surroundings. God's voice is not something we often perceive directly. Rather, we perceive it by noticing how our perception of everything else changes in response.

WALKING THE TALK

People of the emerging Christian faith are people who have reclaimed the ancient commitment to prayer. A half hour or more per day is spent listening more than talking. Prayer matters more than television and is as interesting and endlessly creative as sex.

Emerging Christianity reclaims as well the ancient Rule of Love for discerning scriptural authority. Christians of the emerging faith refuse to recognize any passage or interpretation that moves us away from the love commanded by Jesus. They seek to uncover the deep truths of Scripture even as they may question the historicity of certain stories and events. This is what it means to take Scripture seriously and authoritatively but not literally.

AFFIRMATION

three

Celebrating the God whose Spirit pervades and
whose glory is reflected in all of God's Creation,
including the earth and its ecosystems, the
sacred and secular, the Christian and
non-Christian, the human and non-human

As CHRISTIANS, WE SEEK to act as righteous stewards of the earth
and its ecosystems. We celebrate the reflections of the Creator's
glory in both the sacred and secular, human and non-human,
Christian and non-Christian.

WE AFFIRM that the Path of Jesus is found where Christ's followers act as caring stewards of the earth, and where the presence of
the living Christ is celebrated wherever Christ's spirit manifests itself, transcending all preconceived human categories.

WE CONFESS that we have stepped away from this Path when we
have ignored our role as stewards of the earth, or have interpreted
Scripture in a way that fails to account for the sacredness of the
earth or the integrity of its ecosystems. We have further moved away
whenever we have claimed that the glorification and praise of God
is limited only to that which is consciously and overtly Christian.

*God writes the Gospel not in the Bible alone, but also
on trees, and in the flowers and clouds and stars.*

—Attributed to Martin Luther

"I just don't get how you can be so concerned about the environment when you're a Christian minister." So queried Jake, a twenty-something visitor to my office who has been so strongly interested in the environment since high school that he has stopped going to his family's church altogether and has attended the "Church of the Desert Arroyos," the "Church of the Mountain Lakes," and the "Church of the Tall Pines" pretty much every Sunday since.

Jake called me one day out of the blue saying he'd heard his parents excitedly talking about the Walk Across America I was helping organize with CrossWalk America (http://www. CrossWalkAmerica.org). Having flirted with the idea of walking across the country himself ("just for kicks"), he asked his parents why a Christian organization would be motivated to do it. His parents handed him a copy of the Phoenix Affirmations. Jake said he nearly fell off his chair when he read Affirmation 3, with its assertion that Christian love of God includes caring for the environment.

"Isn't that, like, a major break with Christianity? Aren't you leading people away from their faith?"

"Why do you say that?"

"Well, the Bible commands humans to subdue the earth and have dominion over it, and Christians have been doing so for thousands of years. That's why we have so much environmental devastation today. I had some Christian friends in college who went to some sort of Christian conference or rally once and came back all concerned about my environmental advocacy work. They said the environmental movement is part of a satanic plot to divert people's attention from the spiritual world to the material world. They said environmentalists are just secular humanists trying to cast doubt on God's power to provide for our needs by suggesting that the earth's resources are limited. When I tried showing them the hard facts about the state of the environment, they changed their tune and said that the world isn't going to last much longer anyhow. They said Jesus is going to come back and take believers out of this world. 'Christians are here to play, not to stay,' they said."

Jake apparently noticed my grimace just then. "You don't agree with this?"

"I'd say, 'Hell no!' but your friends might interpret that as a sign that I'm hooked up with the devil," I said.

"So you think the whole thing about subduing the earth and Jesus coming back in the nick of time is a bunch of bunk?"

"I think it's one more sign that Christians have lost touch with their own scriptures. We're no longer reading Scripture with sensitivity to the context in which they were written. We live in the McBible era. People think they can just pull up to the drive-thru window of faith, order a passage or two to meet their needs, and be on their way. Sometimes I think people would be surprised to learn that the phrase 'Would you like fries with that?' isn't in the Bible."

"So you think the Bible is actually environmentally friendly?"

"I think the Bible is *God*-friendly. If care for the earth was the top priority in the Bible, then I wouldn't have much hope either for the earth or Christianity's role in protecting it. However, the heavens and the earth are understood to be God's Creation. They are the subject of God's loving care and intimate attention. The Bible claims that God is so intimately involved with the natural order that to behold God's Creation is to behold God's very Self."[1] Seeing the earth simply as a stockpile of resources to be used in whatever way humanity pleases is not simply bad environmental stewardship but bad theology as well. In biblical terms, it is nothing short of blasphemy against God. Blasphemy is no small matter in the Bible!"

"That makes sense to me," Jake acknowledged, "but I think a lot of Christians would disagree with you. They say we're supposed to subdue and dominate the earth like Genesis says."

"Back to McBible theology," I said. "When the Book of Genesis was written, there was no environmental crisis. Or rather, the environmental crisis was not about the environment being threatened by human beings. It was about human beings being threatened by the environment. You're a hiker, aren't you?"

"Yes, I get out into the wilderness two or three weekends a month."

"When you go out for the weekend, do you take a tent with you?"

"Yes."

"Do you take a camp stove and flashlight?"

"Of course."

"How about protective clothing, sunscreen, and survival gear—like a fishing line and hook, a knife, water purification tablets, and the like?"

"I have all those things."

"And I would imagine you don't go into the wilderness with all this gear for the purpose of raping and pillaging the earth."

"Are you kidding?" Jake winced. "I go out to *appreciate* nature. And I practice no-trace hiking. You'd never even know I was there when I leave a campsite."

"Then you are in a good position to 'hear' Genesis in the context in which it was originally heard by the ancients. You take your equipment into the wilderness because without it the wilderness would be a pretty inhospitable place. Your tent allows you to 'subdue' the driving rains and swarming mosquitoes. Your flashlight and camp stove enable you to 'dominate' the powers of darkness and cold. Your fishing hook . . ."

"I get it," Jake interrupted. "When you put it that way, I'm doing a lot of 'dominating and subduing' when I'm out there. I do it to survive, not harm."

"And I would guess that all the 'dominating and subduing' you do also allow you to kick back and enjoy and appreciate nature."

"That's why I go out. I feel closer to God out there than I do in church."

"Now you know why the Bible is so eloquent about the intimate relationship between God and nature even as it affirms humanity's limited role in 'dominating and subduing' for survival. The ancients would have been as aghast as you and I are at the way certain Christians disrespect the environment. Again, they would have called it blasphemy, not faith."

"Then what about all this talk about not having to worry about protecting the environment because Jesus is coming again?" Jake asked.

"First of all," I said, "according to the Gospel of John, Jesus has *already* returned and is still with us to this day in the form of the Holy Spirit. But that's a conversation for another time. Let's assume that Jesus is coming back yet again—a *Third* Coming, so to speak. If this is the case, then Christians have *even more* reason to be enthusiastic about conservation, not less."

"How so?" asked Jake, unconvinced.

"Jesus told his disciples that no one knew the day or the hour he'd return—not even Jesus himself. He also told them a story about how to prepare for his coming. There are ten bridesmaids who go out to wait for his arrival at the edge of town carrying oil lamps to light his way. Five of the bridesmaids are wise, and five are foolish. The foolish ones are so sure they know the time of the bridegroom's arrival that they fail to make adequate provision in case there's a delay—like bringing extra oil. The wise ones, on the other hand, carefully fill extra flasks with oil just in case. Of course, there is a delay, and they all fall asleep with their lamps burning as they wait. Late that night, someone shouts, 'Here he is! Come out to meet the bridegroom!' (The bridegroom stands for Jesus when he returns.) Of course, by now the oil in everyone's lamps is nearly gone. As the wise bridesmaids refill their lamps, the foolish ones plead, 'Give us some of your oil. Our lamps are going out!' The wise bridesmaids respond, 'No way! There won't be enough for both you and us. You'd better go back and purchase more oil from the merchants.'

"I've always wondered how many merchants were selling oil in the middle of the night! In any case, as the foolish bridesmaids trot off to purchase oil, the bridegroom arrives and the five wise bridesmaids accompany him to the wedding banquet, lighting his way. Later, the foolish bridesmaids arrive demanding entrance to the banquet hall. But the bridegroom replies, 'Truly I tell you, I do not know you.'

"Jesus concludes this story by saying, 'Keep awake, therefore, for you know neither the day nor the hour.'"

Jake saw the point immediately. "Those college friends of mine who were so concerned about me for trying to preserve the earth's resources were like the foolish bridesmaids. They didn't care about conservation because they were so sure Jesus would arrive any day! What if Jesus doesn't return for another thousand years or so? I wonder how they'd feel about 'Here to play, not to stay' then!"

"Jesus has stern words for those who assume they know more about God's timing than even he does."

Jake thought for a moment and then asked, "Do you think enough Christians will take their own scriptures seriously enough to do something about the environment before it's destroyed completely? Quite frankly, I don't see much chance of that."

"I wish I knew, Jake," I answered. "But just as it's foolish to assume that Jesus is coming back the day after tomorrow and thus give up on the environment, it's also unwise in my view to assume that the environment will be destroyed the day after tomorrow and thus give up on Jesus. Both the earth and the Christian faith may very well be around a lot longer than any of us think. It's best to invest our energy in bringing them into harmony with one another while we still can."

Jake left that day feeling a bit better about the Christian faith. I still haven't seen him in church—at least not mine. I suspect that he continues to attend the "Church of the Desert Arroyos" and the "Church of the Mountain Lakes" on Sunday mornings. I wish he'd come around once in a while and worship with us or any other church that takes Affirmation 3 seriously. He would discover a whole community of people of faith who love and respect the environment. Until then, I imagine that he experiences the God he meets out in the lakes and mountains a bit differently than he did before.

WALKING THE TALK

Environmental stewardship is a basic part of walking the Path of Jesus. Given that in the last century, human beings have consumed more of the world's resources than in all of history before that since the dawn of civilization, I suspect that God is calling many to move beyond personal environmental stewardship into communal environmental activism.

Faith-based environmental activism is a bit different from activism without faith connections. The goals and objectives may be similar—and people of faith can certainly join hands and work fruitfully with people of no faith at all for the sake of the environment (and for the sake of friendship). However, the motivation behind faith-based work is different. Environmental activism is motivated by love for God, not simply love for the environment. This does *not* mean that love for God is primary and love for the environment is secondary. It means that love for God integrally includes love for the environment and vice versa. They are part of a seamless whole. Just as one would not look at one's best friend who happens to be the parent and say, "I love you primarily and your child secondarily," so we look at God and God's Creation saying, "I love you both with one love."

Many Christians may agree with Affirmation 3 that loving God includes "celebrating the God whose Spirit pervades and glory is reflected in the earth and its ecosystems . . . the human and nonhuman," yet some may hiccup over the part about including the "the sacred and secular, the Christian and non-Christian." As one person once asked when she learned that my church had played a Pearl Jam song in worship one Sunday, "How can a Christian church bring non-Christian music into sacred space?" Yet if we can affirm that the hills and mountains, the lakes and streams, the flora and fauna somehow bear witness to God's glory and wisdom—even though none of them has any awareness of God (at least as we understand God)— how can we then claim otherwise for human beings? If God created human beings in God's image and likeness, can they not reflect God's glory and wisdom even if they may not be aware of the God of our understanding? If we can affirm with Psalm 96:12 that a group of trees in the forest can somehow be singing joyously to God, then we can surely affirm that a group of rock musicians is capable of doing the same, whether they're aware of it or not.

four

Expressing our love in worship that is as sincere, vibrant, and artful as it is scriptural

As Christians, we strive to respond to God's artistry in Creation by integrating the arts in worship, education, and proclamation. We encourage the reclaiming of artistry and artistic expression in all Christian endeavors, both personal and communal.

We affirm that the Path of Jesus is found where Christ's followers make sincere and vibrant worship of God as central to the life of their community as Jesus did. We further affirm artistic expression as a way of reflecting God's creativity, joy, and prophetic voice in what may be seen, heard, felt, tasted, sung, and spoken.

We confess that we have moved away from Christ's Path when we have failed to make worship the product of our best efforts to experience and express love for God, neighbor, and self in community with others. We have moved farther from this Path when we have considered the arts as trivial or merely tangential to the life of a mature Christian community.

Why do we people in churches seem like cheerful, brainless tourists on a packaged tour of the Absolute? . . . On the whole, I do not find Christians, outside of the catacombs, sufficiently sensible of conditions. Does anyone have the foggiest idea what sort of power we so blithely invoke? Or as I suspect, does no one believe a word of it? The churches are children playing on the floor with their chemistry sets, mixing up a batch of TNT to kill a Sunday morning.

It is madness to wear ladies' straw hats and velvet hats to church; we should all be wearing crash helmets. Ushers should issue life preservers and signal flares; they should lash us to our pews. For the sleeping god may wake someday and take offense, or the waking god may draw us out to where we can never return.

—Annie Dillard, *Teaching a Stone to Talk*

You probably wouldn't expect that a chapter on worship in the emerging Christian faith would take its cue from an ancient Hebrew story from the Book of Leviticus about the death of two priests. Leviticus has the peculiar distinction of being simultaneously the weirdest and most boring book of the entire Bible.

I think you'll find this particular story rather exciting, however. In Leviticus 9 and 10, Aaron and his sons, Nadab and Abihu, have just been ordained as Israel's very first priests. They have performed the necessary offerings, have been anointed by Moses with oil and blood, and have remained inside something called the "tent of meeting" for seven days in preparation for their first sacrifice. The "tent of meeting," or Tabernacle, was a movable worship structure used by the Israelites during their travels from Egypt to the Promised Land. It is said that a pillar of fire would guide the Israelites through the Sinai wilderness, halting in certain places where they would make camp, erect the structure, and wait until the fire moved again. When it moved, they'd disassemble everything and follow the fiery pillar farther along their route.

After the seven days of preparation, Aaron and his sons emerge from the tent and offer their sacrifices to God on behalf of Israel. A strong current of anticipation fills the air as the newly consecrated priests perform their prescribed duties flawlessly. After sacrificing the sin offering, the burnt offering, and the offering of well-being, Aaron blesses the people and comes down from the altar. There is anxious silence as Moses and Aaron reenter the tent of meeting. Are they meeting with God in there? Are they praying? Are they comparing notes? The time for speculation is abruptly over as Moses and Aaron reappear at the mouth of the tent and bless the people one more time. Suddenly, the "glory of God" flashes before everyone's eyes. A fire shoots straight out of the tent and devours every last bit of sacrificial food on the altar.

The people erupt in wild celebration! They have precisely followed the ritual and now they behold the fruit of their labor: God's fiery glory. This is the way it's supposed to work, according to Leviticus. The ritual, the liturgy, the *Tradition* forms a kind of human-made vessel into which God's wild, fiery, unstructured Spirit comes and meets with the people. Tradition and experience, form and function, the mediation of the priests and the immediacy of God's Spirit join together in a "match made in heaven," and the people rejoice.

But perhaps there was a little too much rejoicing that day, a bit too much confidence in the beautiful new relationship between God and the people. I can imagine what might have been running through the minds of Nadab and Abihu. "Wow!" they're thinking, "We did it! We brought God into our midst! Yes!"

As the smoke clears, Nadab turns to Abihu asking, "But where's God now?"

"Gone, I guess," answers Abihu.

"But Abi, we could bring God back again if we had a little something to offer. If we find some coals, we could make an incense offering and maybe bring God back!"

"That's right!" shouts Abihu excitedly.

Quickly, they fill their censers with glowing coals. Throwing incense on them, they raise their censers in front of the tent and await God's fire. Indeed, the fire returns, but not as the two young priests had intended. We read, "They offered strange fire before the Lord, such as [God] had not commanded them. And fire came out from the presence of the Lord and consumed them, and they died before the Lord" (Leviticus 10:1–2). As one commentator puts it, "Inspired by a fire, they made a fire, and promptly they were destroyed by the inspiring fire."[1]

What went wrong? Were the boys simply standing in the wrong spot at the wrong time? Was their incineration the product of God's wrath that would have caught up with them no matter where they stood? We're not told. What we *are* told is that the "strange fire" they offered was not commanded by God. *Strange* here means "unauthorized," "foreign." It wasn't part of the plan, the structure, the Tradition.

It would appear that the young priests were a bit too zealous about making God stick around. In their enthusiasm, they overrode the boundaries of the prescribed ritual. These were protective boundaries—boundaries set up to shield the people from the awesome presence of God. The ritual was meticulously followed not in order to make God come, as Nadab and Abihu seemed to think, but to withstand the force of God's coming. Let me repeat that thought: The ritual was followed not in order to make God come but *to withstand the force of God's coming.*

In a sense, ritual dampens God's presence, softens the impact. It diffuses the blow by absorbing it in a host of minute details and procedures. What the Book of Leviticus is practically screaming at us to understand is that God's presence is so potent that if we don't follow a ritual—a Tradition—very carefully, we won't know what hit us. The young priests stepped outside the ritual parameters and in so doing lost their protection. They had become a little too comfortable about being in God's presence. They didn't realize that God's Spirit cannot be tamed.

Most who read the ninth chapter of Leviticus—not to mention the eight chapters of ritual instruction that precede it—find it dull and boring. And it is! We find ourselves thinking, "God doesn't need all those sacrifices, anointings, and cleansings in order to be present with people. Those things are just the relics of ancient superstitions." But if one of the authors of Leviticus were here today, he would probably say we've got it backward. *God* doesn't need the ritual. *We* do. Experiencing God is like standing next to a raging fire. Israel's traditions operated like a fire protection barrier designed to contain the fire just enough so that they could be warmed and illuminated by the flame without being burned. They were playing with fire by calling on God, and they knew enough to take the proper precautions.

Their ritual was a way of *seeking* God's presence, not avoiding it. In effect, Leviticus says, "Here's a way you can build a fire protection wall around you so that when God comes, you and the fire can coexist without your being consumed." But it also says, "Beware: if manufacturer's directions are not followed, the warrantee is void!"

This is helpful instruction. Rather than telling us, "Stay away from the fire! ("Stay away from God"), the authors of Leviticus are showing us a way to safely draw near. We may no longer feel compelled to sacrifice sheep and oxen, but the principle still holds true: without the structure that a living Tradition provides, encountering God can be overwhelming, perhaps even dangerous.

Yet if taken too far, the message of Leviticus can easily degenerate into something like "Don't ever go messing with the Tradition! Do exactly as we say and don't question it, or you'll be sorry!" The problem with this message is that it fails to take account of the fact that the Spirit of God doesn't stay in one place for very long. God's fire in Leviticus is on the move, leading the people to the Promised Land, and it continues to be on the move today. As Jesus once observed, "The wind [or in our case, the fire] blows where it chooses, and you hear the sound of it, but you do not know where it comes from or where it goes" (John 3:8).

In other words, if the fire of God's Spirit is burning in our midst, there is no better way to coexist with it than within a Tradition. But if the fire's burning elsewhere, we'd best disassemble our Tradition, take whatever is still usable, and move with it, like the Israelites did.

Surely, the Pharisees would have compared Jesus to Nadab and Abihu. They would have seen Jesus as a young buck who was too confident, too optimistic about the tameness of God. "Don't leap the barrier, Jesus, or you'll be sorry!" they would say. "Watch out! You're healing on the Sabbath! Be careful! You're mixing with unclean people. Take heed! You're forgiving sins with no authority! God's Spirit is a raging fire, and you'll get burned if you change the Tradition! Just do what we tell you to do, and you and your followers will be safe."

In effect, Jesus was telling them, "You're right! God's Spirit really *is* a raging fire. The Tradition really *can* protect us from the heat. Only the fire is no longer burning where you think it is. If you want to feel the warmth of the flame, tear down the barrier of your Tradition, bring what's still salvageable, and follow me. I'll take you into the Fire Zone."

There is bitter irony here. Nadab and Abihu broke with a Tradition that in its day was located right where the flame of God was burning brightest—and were killed by that flame.

Jesus broke with the same Tradition, which was by that time located far from the flame—and was killed by those charged with keeping people safe from burns.

Does this strange passage from Leviticus suggest anything regarding our situation today? As we swiftly move into the third millennium, much in our society is in a state of flux. Science is changing our basic understandings of the world and our place in it, and ethical notions once thought to be universal and time-less are eroding or contested. Although it is hard sometimes not to become mesmerized by the negative effects of such rapid change, those who have eyes to see recognize that God is con-tinuing to shed new light in a darkened world. The fire is mov-ing. How do we respond?

We could react to all the changes in our world by casting off our Tradition and embracing each and every hot new trend that comes along. But as Nadab and Abihu found, touching the fire without the shield of a Tradition can be hazardous. On the other hand, we could respond by becoming firmly entrenched in our existing Tradition. But when the fire has moved on, it is just as deadly to stay within a fixed Tradition as it is to move un-protected into the flame.

Happily, there is an alternative. Instead of casting off Tradi-tion, or rigidly adhering to every letter of it, we can choose to take our Tradition with us into the Fire Zone, seeking the heat with a little protection. We don't cast away hymnbooks—we create new ones; we don't adamantly cling to literalistic interpretations of Scripture—we learn to read it with new eyes. From within our Tradition, we can faithfully incorporate new scientific insights and engage social and ethical challenges. We can be open to the world, unafraid of being on the front lines of cultural transition. We can be a creative and guiding voice amid these upheavals because we have a living Tradition through which to comprehend, assess, and assimilate them. Throughout many periods of history, this has been what the church has done best.

What we need now is to be *more* connected to our Tradition, not less. We need to be studying the Bible, church history, and the basic tenets of our faith in order to get profoundly in touch with the spiritual fire that guides it. But at the same time, we need to stay open more earnestly than ever to the direction in which the flame is moving and be willing to follow where it leads. This is the way we will move through the third millennium if the Christian faith is to survive and prosper. We seek the fire and follow. With the shield of a living, dynamic Tradition embracing us, it is not the consuming flame but its warmth and illumination that will touch our souls.

WALKING THE TALK

During the last few decades, there has been no small amount of controversy in Christian churches over worship style. As those who advocated for maintaining "traditional" worship and those preferring "contemporary" forms struggled against one another, many started referring to the conflict as the "worship wars." Churches within the emerging Christian faith, however, appear to be moving beyond the worship wars. They are discovering a "third way" in worship, one that cannot easily be categorized as either traditional or contemporary. It neither abandons Tradition nor clings to it. The third way very much appears to be a dismantling of the Tradition for the purpose not of abandonment but of reerecting it in a new place. This probably explains why these churches tend to be highly resistant to calling their worship "traditional," "contemporary," or "blended." Instead, they refer to what they do as "ancient-future worship" or "emergent worship" or "experiential worship" or "incarnational worship." This last term, to me, best describes what's going on.

Although incarnational worship takes a very wide variety of forms, several common threads hold it together. First, it is centered on *experiencing* God incarnate in everyday life more than *learning about* God. If the worship theme is, for instance, "God, our Creator," the purpose of the service is not conceived as primarily teaching the congregation that God is the Creator and why it should matter. Rather, worship leaders start with the question, "How do people experience God as Creator in everyday life?" The whole world then becomes a palate from which leaders work to open people up to experiencing God as Creator in worship. The idea is not to manufacture an experience but rather to open participants to the possibility of an experience. Incarnational worship operates on the assumption that God's Spirit really is alive and well in this world and will not hesitate to stir the soul if people's hearts are open and attentive. This assumption is made in theologically liberal churches as well as more conservative ones.

Second, incarnational worship tends to be mediated through a wide variety of multisensory elements, which may range from quite ancient to postmodern. Participants are as likely to experience worship through smell, taste, and physical touch as they are through sight and sound. There is frequently an emphasis on prayer and contemplative forms of Scripture reading, such as *lectio divina*. At the same time, these elements may be interwoven with film clips, jazz or rock music, and hands-on artistic creation.

Emphasis on the arts and artistic expression, in fact, is a third unifying element in incarnational worship. Practitioners of incarnational worship feel that worship should be as artistic as it is scripturally based. It would not be at all surprising, in this regard, to find churches of the emerging Christian faith eventually reclaiming the church's more ancient role of supporting the arts and artistic expression even as it does so in a new way.

Finally, incarnational worship is frequently created by clusters of people rather than by single individuals or pairs. Pastors work with a worship team made up of both clergy and laity for generating ideas, creating the service, and carrying it off. In this we may be seeing the Reformation principle of the Priesthood of All Believers practiced on a larger and deeper scale than it ever has been before (for more on this, see Affirmation 12).

five

꧁

Engaging people authentically, as Jesus did, treating all
as creations made in God's very image, regardless
of race, gender, sexual orientation, age, physical
or mental ability, nationality, or economic class

AS CHRISTIANS, WE WELCOME persons of every race, gender, sexual orientation, age, physical and mental ability, nationality, and economic class into the full life of our community.

WE AFFIRM that the Path of Jesus is found where Christ's followers uplift and celebrate the worth and integrity of all people as created in God's very image and likeness. We further affirm that Christ's Path includes treating people authentically rather than as mere categories or classes, challenging and inspiring all people to live according to their high identity.

WE CONFESS that we have stepped away from this Path whenever we have failed to recognize the essential goodness of God's Creation by treating some classes of human beings as more godly than others. We have moved farther from Christ's Path when we have treated people superficially, as objects to be used rather than human beings with depth and distinction.

Ecclesia reformata simper reformanda

(A reformed church always reforming)

—Cornerstone of the sixteenth-century
Protestant Reformation

Most of the great revolutions in Christianity since its earliest beginnings have been related in one way or another to the spirit of Affirmation 5. There is a drive deep in the heart of the faith that inspires and sometimes torments Christians to extend the circle of God's love and compassion beyond their immediate comfort zone. This drive originates at the base of a cross where all confidence in human achievement, righteousness, and knowledge is lost. It extends through the mouth of an empty tomb where despite all odds and expectations, love walks out alive and well. The Christian church has not always lived up to its call to walk with Jesus on this Path. Sometimes, in fact, Jesus has walked alone as the church has taken the stance of Pilate, naively washing its hands of culpability even as it nails love once again to the cross. Hence the recurring need for revolution. Yet as William Sloane Coffin observes, the church cannot repress its drive to extend the circle of love and compassion indefinitely:

> The Church may distort Jesus into a white middle-class pillar of American respectability; it may pervert his image into that of a religious Babbitt pushing the cult of successfulness; it may distort and pervert his image, but the Church

cannot forget Jesus. And in spite of its best efforts to domes-
ticate that Jesus, the Church knows and frequently fears that
his message will be rediscovered. The Church cannot help
but keep the name in circulation, and where the name is
remembered there is hope.[1]

Today, many Christians are in fact remembering the name
they have kept in circulation for so long. They feel called to move
beyond their immediate comfort zone to recognize that the guest
list for God's party is a lot larger than previously imagined.

I am one of those Christians who used to believe God's
guest list was much smaller than I do now. The circle that rep-
resented my most significant growing edge and source of dis-
comfort was with the gay and lesbian community. As a straight
male, I had a very difficult time comprehending how anyone
could fall in love with someone of the same sex without it being
the product of some sort of perversion. While I have always
advocated inclusion of gays and lesbians in the community of
faith, I still used to believe that homosexuality is intrinsically
sinful. I felt that since the church is a place for sinners, homosexuals should be welcomed to church in the hopes that they,
like the rest of us, could find forgiveness and healing of their
sins. I was therefore not just suspicious of but downright vexed
by claims by some Christians that the church should not only
be open to but affirming of homosexuals and homosexuality. To
me, this was simply taking things too far. I suspected it was the
product of liberal political correctness run amok.

I had no idea that the truth could be so different.

What changed my understanding? It was certainly not a desire to be more politically correct! Rather, it was Jesus. Jesus acting, at first, in and through a person named John, followed by many others.

John was a person I admired and respected greatly who one day "came out" in great fear and trembling to a group of friends of whom I was one. John's revelation shook my world so profoundly that I knew I needed to explore more deeply the roots of my beliefs. He was the first homosexual I had ever known, or at least the first I'd ever known to be homosexual. John simply did not fit any of my preconceived notions. He was a person of faith and a model of love and compassion. He had the highest ethical sensibilities of anyone I knew. The juxtaposition between what I expected of a homosexual and the one I suddenly discovered I knew and admired bothered me greatly.

I did not change my views on homosexuality right away. I don't tend to just hop on any new revelation and go with it. I have to test it, prod it, pull it, stretch it, throw it away and see if it comes back. My present views took shape over a period of several years during which I made a point of getting to know homosexuals and my own scriptures better. Much to my surprise, and despite my protests, Jesus kept showing up in the most surprising places! Both the scriptures I was reading and the gays and lesbians I was getting to know made me recognize that there is much more to faith and sexuality than I had realized. It ended up changing my way of thinking.[2]

But enough about me. Let's turn to Scripture, to Jesus, and to the revolution he started. In what follows, we'll trace a thread of biblical and Christian history that concerns far more than one's views about homosexuality. It is a thread that lies at the heart of Affirmation 5 and pretty much every revolution that has taken place since the beginning of Christianity. The thread begins with the apostle Peter throwing a stone into a pond. The stone and pond are metaphorical, to be sure, but the stone is very large and the ripples very real. They continue to spread across the pond to this very day.

The story is found in the tenth chapter of the Book of Acts. Even in the first century, the story was considered so important that the writer of Acts (Luke, who also wrote the Gospel that bears his name) spends more time on this incident than on any other in the rest of the book, including the story of Paul's conversion.

It starts with Peter praying on the roof of a tanner's house in the seaside town of Joppa. Funny how so many revolutions start with prayer! After praying awhile, Peter starts to get hungry. It's lunchtime. Rather than ending his prayers, as most of us would, Peter continues. Then comes a very strange vision. Peter sees a giant blanket drifting down from the sky suspended by its four corners. On the blanket is spread before him a full array of animals considered "unclean" to Jews and strictly forbidden to consume. Peter's stomach growls. Then Peter hears a voice. To his horror, it says, "Go to it, Peter. Kill and eat. Anything you want."

"Hold on," Peter answers. "God, you're playing with my mind! I've never in my entire life eaten anything unclean. This can't be right."

And how *could* it be right? The laws of Leviticus 11 have been etched on Peter's heart since childhood, marking out which animals are "clean" and authorized for eating and which are "unclean" and forbidden. He knows, for instance, that cows are "clean" because they chew the cud and have a divided hoof. Pigs are "unclean" because although they have a divided hoof, they don't chew cud. To consume what is "unclean" is considered an abomination by God. It clearly says so in Scripture.

"I'm not going to do it," Peter says, probably suspecting that God is testing his loyalty. The voice responds, "What God has declared clean you must not call profane." Peter doesn't budge, now likely afraid that it's the devil tempting him. The blanket is lifted back up to the heavens.

To you and me, it may appear that Peter is making something out of nothing. If a voice is telling him to chow down a plate of barbecued pork ribs, what's the big deal? It should be obvious that such things are perfectly fine. But consider Peter's perspective. Peter's Jewish. All Christians up to this point are Jews who believe that the long-anticipated Messiah had arrived in Jesus. As far as Peter knows, laws governing eating behavior were established by God through Moses since the very beginning of Israelite history, over a thousand years earlier. To really get a sense of what Peter was feeling, imagine yourself seeing the same vision, only it's a blanket piled high with dogs, cats, hamsters, and gerbils. Then a voice tells *you*, "It's chow time!"

The example may seem grotesque, but these animals are all safe to eat. Our revulsion is a product of long-established cultural taboos against eating animals that are normally pets. Now imagine how you would feel if, in addition to your instinctive sense of revulsion, you were convinced that God would be angry if you ate them. If you can feel all this in your gut, you have a sense of how Peter was feeling.

Peter tries his best to ignore the vision and continue his prayers. But again the vision returns. Peter doesn't budge. What is Peter to believe, after all: a voice in his head or Scripture? He buckles down and prays all the harder.

One last time, Peter's prayers are interrupted by a vision of "unclean" animals on the blanket, the command to kill and consume, and the assurance that God has declared them clean. Peter once more replies, "Forget it." The blanket is lifted.

While Peter is worrying about the meaning of the vision, a Roman soldier and two slaves from Caesarea show up asking for Peter. They want him to come and meet with a Roman commander. "Why on earth would *Gentiles*—including a filthy Roman soldier—want to talk with me?" he's probably thinking. As with eating "unclean" foods, associating with or visiting Gentiles was clearly against Jewish law. And he clearly remembers who killed his master, Jesus. Yet a quiet whisper in Peter's head assures him that they've been sent by God and that he should do what they ask. Perhaps softened a bit by the recurring visions, Peter agrees to accompany them back to Caesarea.

Once Peter arrives at the Roman commander's house in Caesarea, either all hell breaks loose or all heaven, depending on your perspective. The commander, named Cornelius, bows down and worships at Peter's feet. "Get up," Peter says. "I'm only a mortal!" Surely this would have struck Peter as one more sign of the baseness of Roman religiosity. "These Romans will worship *anything!*"

As Peter is invited inside, he discovers a whole houseful of Gentiles anxiously waiting to hear him tell them about Jesus. Peter acknowledges a bit nervously that his being there is highly illegal according to Jewish law but proceeds to speak of his faith and experience of Jesus' ongoing and transformative love. As Peter speaks, a growing sense of awe and wonder descends on the household. Pretty soon, everyone's in a frenzy, shouting amens and hallelujahs and generally raising the roof with God's praises. Peter and his Jewish companions struggle to make sense of what's going on. These Gentiles are responding in the same ways the Jews have when the Holy Spirit has come upon them. But no one ever taught Peter and his companions that the Spirit could awaken the hearts of Gentiles. In fact, they'd always been taught otherwise. If the Holy Spirit has actually come into Gentiles, Peter reasons, it could only mean that God is welcoming them within the circle of faith. Finally, Peter gets it: the vision in Joppa was not simply about food. It was about *people*. "What God has declared clean you must not call profane." So Peter extends to the crowd the rite of baptism, which is the basic initiation rite into the Christian faith. They readily accept, becoming the first official non-Jewish members of the family of Jesus.

All is well and good after this until Christian leaders hear of what Peter has done. Peter is summoned immediately to appear before a council in Jerusalem. *The Message* Bible version of Acts 10:34–36 conveys what happens better than I can:

> Peter fairly exploded with his good news: "It's God's own truth, nothing could be plainer: God plays no favorites! It makes no difference who you are or where you're from— if you want God and are ready to do as he says, the door is open. The Message he sent to the children of Israel—that through Jesus Christ everything is being put together again—well, he's doing it everywhere, among everyone.

It is hard for us today to imagine, but if Peter and others like him had not won this debate convincing their peers to look beyond the clear words of Scripture and a thousand years of Tradition and into the very heart of God, almost none of us would be Christians. The greatest struggle in the first-century church by far was not between Christians and Jews but between Christian Jews who felt that God and Tradition had put a giant period in God's Word and Christian Jews who insisted that God had inserted a comma. God was calling them to move beyond their comfort zone and welcome those whom God had already embraced.

Can you imagine the guts Peter and his fellow believers must have had to stand up for the Gentiles? Can you imagine how many times Peter must have second-guessed himself as people angrily quoted Scripture at him about committing an abomination and incurring God's wrath? This is the unfortunate underbelly of every story of revolution in the Christian faith. We look back with the benefit of hindsight and assume that it must have been so easy—even joyful—to stand with those outside the traditional circle of faith. In reality, there is plenty of joy but also plenty of pain at the heart of the struggle. The greater joy is left to future generations who inherit the fruits of their ancestors.

The Protestant Reformation of the sixteenth century was one of the inheritors of the ripple effect of what happened in the first century. Once again, many people within the church, which had distorted and domesticated Jesus almost beyond recognition, were beginning to remember and reawaken to his Path. The best known among these was German theologian Martin Luther. Luther is said to have nailed a list of ninety-five theses, or complaints against the Catholic church, to the door of the Wittenberg Cathedral in a bold effort to push the church past its familiar comfort zones into the ever-widening sphere of transformative grace. So deep and sweeping were the reforms Luther called for that the church erupted. Soon Luther, who had sought not to leave the church but to reform it, was tossed out. He wasn't nearly as fortunate in his reception by his peers as Peter, whose views at least prevailed with the Jerusalem council. Luther spent much of his remaining life staying one step ahead of people who sought to kill him.

The movement Luther engendered created its own ripple effect, rapidly spreading both geographically and philosophically.

Protestant churches are the inheritors of this ripple. Lutheran theologian Larry Rasmussen captures its essence:

> The Protestant Reformers urged people to reread scriptures and tradition through different lenses and write new confessions they would stake their lives on. They encouraged clergy to leave behind some of their ordination vows (celibacy, in this case). They drastically revised the number and meaning of the sacraments, they re-crafted the liturgy, and they composed stirring new hymns and songs—some from popular music. Not least, they democratized the church in startling ways, literally gave it a new language and unleashed the laity to take responsibility for their lives, rituals, neighbors, theology and conscience. They even chose a controversial biblical theme—the justification of the *un*godly—as the great good news story.[3]

The ripples of this great Reformation continue, provoking major and minor revolutions of spirit in their wake. In the nineteenth century, the ripple inspired Christians to work for the liberation of slaves in the United States and to ordain the first woman minister in America.[4] In both cases, Christians had to see beyond clear biblical teachings condoning slavery and the subordination of women as well as nearly two thousand years of tradition in order to follow Jesus from the empty tomb into the streets. In the twentieth century, the ripple inspired Christians to welcome divorcees into full church membership and allow remarriage after divorce. It also inspired Christians to work for full equality in the eyes of civil law for women and racial minorities. Once again, Christians had to see beyond certain parts of Scripture and lengthy Christian tradition into the heart and soul of their faith in order to follow Jesus.

If Christian history teaches us anything at all, it demonstrates that it takes three things to move out of our comfort zone: a cross, an empty tomb, and the will to follow Jesus through both. This is never quite as easy as it seems it should be. We can't break through barriers of human awareness and pride using achievement, knowledge, or ability by themselves. As with Luther and Peter, we are called at the foot of the cross to surrender our desire for esteem in the beloved community, our thirst for personal security, and even the assurance that both Scripture and Tradition are fully on our side. Indeed, we are called to surrender everything.

Yet at the empty tomb, one discovers that when we surrender everything, we do not lose but instead gain. "Those who lose their life for my sake will find it," says Jesus (Matthew 16:25). To walk with Jesus on the other side of the cross is to enter a realm where transformative love works miracles for Gentiles excluded from the faith community, for laity excluded from taking faith into their own hands, for slaves held in bondage, for women held in subordination, for divorcees prohibited from remarrying, for racial minorities excluded from a white world, and for gays and lesbians blocked from full participation in the straight world. In short, it is a realm where love works miracles for the darnedest people—including you and me.

WALKING THE TALK

Where is the next ripple inspiring Christians to push through the barriers that constrain God's Realm? We seem to be in one of those periods in Christian history where the ripples are pushing against many barriers at once. If we truly wish to follow where Jesus appears to be walking, those who come after us may very well look back at our time and identify it as the precursor to the next Great Reformation — which would mean that we are living in a time of great crisis and great opportunity.

The full inclusion of gays and lesbians into the life of the church, and indeed the life of the nation, appears to be one of those barriers Christ is calling us to push through. To be sure, this is just one of several areas where Christians are called into greater discipleship. However, this is the area where Scripture and Tradition pose the largest barriers to following in Christ's footsteps.

This is not to imply that there is more Scripture or deeper Tradition to overcome with respect to gays and lesbians than there was for, say, slaves or women. In the days when these were pressing issues, Christians had to work through even greater amounts of Scripture and more deeply entrenched Tradition than we face today.[5] As a society, we have not yet processed these matters to the extent that our predecessors did with their issues.

Christian denominations have spent years of study on the nuances of Scripture and Tradition, and still we are at a stalemate. This is because it is impossible to follow the ripples of

Peter's stone throw if we focus solely on Scripture and Tradition. As Luther would tell us, one must focus on Christ. It is time for the church to reawaken to Jesus and follow him on the Path where he joyfully and unapologetically beckons us.

six

Standing, as Jesus does, with the outcast and oppressed, the denigrated and afflicted, seeking peace and justice with or without the support of others

AS CHRISTIANS, WE ADVOCATE and care for those who experience oppression and poverty, either physically or spiritually, in our faith communities, our country, and the world. We recognize the local congregation as the primary context for offering such care, even as we seek to extend it beyond our faith communities into the wider world.

WE AFFIRM that the Path of Jesus is found where Christ's followers honor the essential unity of spirit and matter by connecting worship and theology with concrete acts of justice and righteousness, kindness, and humility, with or without the support of others.

WE CONFESS that we have moved away from this Path when we have suggested that Christianity is concerned with only the spiritual in contrast to the material or vice versa. We have moved further away when we have celebrated blessings given by God without also acknowledging responsibilities that come with blessing.

> *If the debtor be insolvent to serve creditors, let his body*
> *be cut in pieces on the third market day. It may be cut into*
> *more or fewer pieces with impunity. Or, if his creditors consent*
> *to it, let him be sold to foreigners beyond the Tiber.*
>
> — From Table III of the Twelve Tables, centerpiece
> of the constitution of the Roman Republic (c. 450 B.C.E.)

Verna is surprisingly youthful for a woman of sixty-three. She started coming to church a couple of years ago, drawn by our jazz worship service. Initially, I took her to be one of Scottsdale's many wealthy widows who spend their days on the golf courses and evenings out on the town dancing with eligible bachelors. I was right about one thing: Verna loves to dance— she's out and about two or three nights a week. Lots of elderly gentlemen have tried to date her. Verna isn't interested. She'll let them buy her a drink and perhaps dinner, but she's still grieving the loss of her husband of thirty-seven years.

Verna came to my office for counseling. She told me a very sad story about how she and her husband had lost nearly everything with the failure of their business and his subsequent illness and death. Just before he died, they had been relying on credit cards to survive, and now she was receiving three to seven calls a day from angry collection agents. And she couldn't seem to shake the loss of her husband. She was considering declaring bankruptcy. She wasn't getting enough to eat and refused to take a handout from the church.

After a few sessions, I finally asked Verna how much she owed on her credit cards. Although I was expecting to hear fifty thousand dollars or more, the answer was ten thousand. To me, that seemed manageable, if Verna could get a part-time job. I suggested that to her.

But Verna wasn't sure; she didn't think she had any skills except dancing. But she enthusiastically agreed to try once I showed her that she could both pay off her debts and have a little extra to live on if she found a job.

When I came back after my summer leave, I met with Verna to find out what had happened. The news was not good. Despite applying at the local Wal-Mart, a score of department stores, and two or three clothing retailers, none of them hired her even though most had initially expressed strong interest in her. When I asked why, she told me that the employers said they'd have to run a credit check before she could start employment.

I could hardly believe my ears. "What does Wal-Mart care if your credit is bad? Last time I heard, aisle clerks weren't handing out financial advice."

"People who have bad credit are considered bigger risks or unreliable, I suppose."

"But risks to what?" I asked, still in shock. "It's not like you were going to be handling money. People with bad credit need jobs more than anyone," I countered, then realized she probably didn't need to hear more. She was downhearted enough.

After Verna left, I made a number of phone calls, still in shock that a widow struggling to pay off her bills and to provide herself three meals a day was being blocked from the workforce. I had no idea how naive I was. Not only did I discover that the practice is prevalent in entry-level retail and wholesale work, but it's rapidly becoming commonplace all the way up the ladder. I had to wonder about all the families who fall on hard times and see their credit ratings suffer. To be sure, there are those who are simply irresponsible with money. However, in more than half of personal bankruptcy cases in the United States, the cause is not irresponsibility but illness.[1] More than three-quarters of these bankruptcies involve middle-class people who are insured at the start of their illness. Over half own a home and have attended college. Personal bankruptcy strikes deep at the heart of our country and affects many hardworking people when their families are already undergoing severe crisis.

So much for the American dream. If the practice of refusing employment to people with poor credit continues, where will we be fifty years from now? If the trend toward reducing health care and other key benefits to those who are employed continues and we persist in refusing to raise the minimum wage to even subsistence levels, what kind of society will we hand on to our children? Instead of finding a Promised Land, will they find we've turned it into the land of Egyptian slavery? What is particularly troubling is that these injustices are not generally created by evil people who care nothing for God or the everyday person but by "good" people trapped in a corrupting system.

To illustrate, suppose that you have been made the new CEO of XYZ Big Box Chain Store. You're not a fat cat drawing a zillion dollars a year in salary and stock options. You're just a hardworking executive who tries to do your best for your company and its employees. But yours is a large company with a million employees in outlets from coast to coast. One day, you pick up an industry journal and read a report that shows that, say, ten percent of the employees at companies like yours tend to have bad credit. It also shows these people are, say, one percent more likely to steal a hundred dollars or more from the company in a year's time and three percent more likely to take two or more sick days than other employees. As you consider the statistics, the implications for your corporation begin to dawn on you.

You take out a calculator and run the numbers: Ten percent of a million employees is one hundred thousand who have bad credit. One percent of these—a thousand employees—are likely to steal a hundred dollars or more. That's a minimum of a hundred thousand dollars cost to the company's bottom line each year. You then run the numbers for sick days and find that these employees could cost your company an extra six thousand employee days per year, which amounts to an extra three hundred thousand dollars. Thus if you do nothing but screen out potential employees with poor credit, you will eventually save the company in the neighborhood of four hundred thousand dollars per year *and* you'll have a workforce that shows up for work more often.

As the CEO, you're a compassionate person who truly wants to help hardworking people who are having trouble. But you also know that your competitors are no longer hiring those with bad credit—they're sending them your way! Your board of directors has not ignored the report either. If you don't act on the report, the board will wonder where your loyalties lie. Are you working for the employees or the stockholders? You are aware that people in the company who are gunning for your position would not hesitate to take a hard line if it meant getting your job. So you can choose to stand up for what you believe in and get replaced by someone who will do what you refused to do, or you can crack down and hope to act as a change agent in some other way.

If the challenges Verna faced were simply the product of corrupt people in high places, we would have little reason to fear as a society. Many people want to do the right thing but are constrained from doing it by the bottom-line practices of the business world. Others, perceiving the implausibility of acting ethically, give up trying from the start, pretending that ethics and business are essentially unrelated.

In this climate, we *do* have something to fear. When the entire system is corrupt, we can no longer hope for personal transformation to solve our problems. The system itself must change. And systemic change far exceeds the capacity of any individual, community, or even large numbers of communities to effect.

How are we as Christians to work for change in a system that completely dwarfs our ability to change as individuals and communities of faith? Although we could all rush out to picket the big chain stores of the world or dash off letters to Congress, I suggest that we also invest energy into getting in touch with the biblical stories of our spiritual ancestors, many of whom struggled faithfully with surprisingly similar issues. When simple stories that crystallize our struggles begin to spark the public imagination, history shows that they can be more powerful change agents than rafts of politicians. In recent history, one may note the simple story of Cindy Sheehan and the son she lost in Iraq. Whether you agree or disagree with her actions or her stance on the war effort, there is no doubt that her story—more than any politician, pundit, or movie star—captivated public interest as she camped outside the president's ranch in Crawford, Texas. The stories of the Bible can act similarly and stay in the public imagination a lot longer, provided that there are people who understand their power and actively share their wisdom.

Consider the story of Amos, for instance. Amos lived in Israel almost three thousand years ago during a time of tremendous prosperity. Due to a number of internal and external political and economic factors, wealth was flowing into the country in amounts rarely seen in the history of biblical Israel. But all this money was not benefiting everyone equally. The rich were getting richer, and the poor were getting poorer. Sound familiar? God asked Amos to deliver a message to the people to address this inequitable situation head on.

Thus says the LORD:
For three transgressions of Israel, and for four,
I will not revoke the punishment;
because they sell the righteous for silver,
and the needy for a pair of sandals—
they who trample the head of the poor into the dust
    of the earth,
and push the afflicted out of the way;

father and son go in to the same girl,
so that my holy name is profaned;
they lay themselves down beside every altar on garments
   taken in pledge;
and in the house of their God they drink wine bought
   with fines they imposed. (Amos 2:6–8)

To understand the essence of God's anger in this passage, it is helpful to know a little Hebrew and something about Jewish tradition. Take the part that reads "they sell the righteous for silver, and the needy for a pair of sandals." This is classic Hebrew poetic parallelism, meaning Amos is not talking about two different kinds of people, the righteous and the needy. Righteous and needy go together, as do silver and sandals. In other words, the righteous needy are being sold for silver and sandals. The part that is translated "for silver" in "sell the righteous for silver" is actually a colloquialism in Hebrew that means "at the going rate." The righteous are being sold "at the going rate"—the rate that is customary or commonly acknowledged as appropriate. The going rate is *not* a pair of sandals, as the passage may imply to the modern reader. Sandals indicate that a legal contract has been made. In ancient Israel, you sealed a deal by swapping a sandal with the other party. That way, if the other party ever tried to claim in a court of law that no deal had been made, you could produce a sandal that fit his foot as evidence.

A similar concept is behind the mention of a cloak at the end of the passage. If a poor person asked you for a temporary loan, promising to pay it when he got paid at the end of the day, you had a legal right to ask him for his cloak as collateral. Because most of the poor had only one cloak, they had high incentive to pay you back, or they would end up sleeping in the cold.

The essence of the passage is that God is angry that people are trampling "the head of the poor into the dust of the earth" and pushing "the afflicted out of the way" and *doing it legally*. They're selling humans into debt slavery at the "going rate" and sealing the deal by perfectly legal means.

One might assume that all this legalized injustice is happening because Israel has strayed from worshiping God, but this is not the case. In fact, it rapidly becomes obvious when one reads the Book of Amos straight through that this is a time of intense religious devotion to Yahweh. Amos' audience is "going to church every Sunday," so to speak. They're celebrating all the religious holidays. They're tithing, eating kosher, and keeping the Sabbath. There is no evidence that the people have gone chasing after other gods or have become religious slouches.

Nevertheless, Yahweh says (in Amos 5:21–27):

I hate, I despise your festivals, and I take no delight in your solemn assemblies. Even though you offer me your burnt offerings and grain offerings, I will not accept them; and the offerings of well-being of your fatted animals I will not look upon. Take away from me the noise of your songs; I will not listen to the melody of your harps. But let justice roll down like waters, and righteousness like an everflowing stream. Did you bring to me sacrifices and offerings the forty years in the wilderness, O house of Israel? You shall take up Sakkuth your king, and Kaiwan your star-god, your images, which you made for yourselves; therefore I will take you into exile beyond Damascus, says the LORD, whose name is the God of hosts.

What God is saying is that despite all Israel's good religious practices—the festivals (to Yahweh), the offerings (to Yahweh), the songs of praise (to Yahweh), and so on—*they might as well be worshiping astral deities if there is no justice in the land for the poor and disenfranchised.*

In Amos' day, his message didn't go over so well. It was only after northern Israel was conquered by the Assyrians and the people there were exiled that people began to think twice about Amos' warnings. Many Christians cringe at the violence attributed to God in the Hebrew scriptures. They believe that the destruction that occurred less than three decades later was the product not of God's will but of human behavior. This may be perfectly true without negating Amos' point. Whether God does it or we do it to ourselves, when the social system becomes infected, leaving the poor with no authentic reason to hope, and when the religious establishment becomes a party to their travail, the biblical faith tells us in no uncertain terms that it is time for those with "eyes to see" and "ears to hear" to stand with Jesus himself on their behalf. It's time to tell and retell our stories, driving them as deeply as possible into the popular imagination, letting our stories of faith and faithfulness inform our actions.

WALKING THE TALK

Stories matter. Although they don't enjoy the popularity of TV shows in America, biblical stories continue to be read and told long after ephemeral TV programs have been forgotten. Biblical stories matter—at least in theory—to the vast majority of Americans who call themselves either Christians or Jews. In the past thirty years, while some Christians have gradually let go of storytelling in favor of direct political action, others have not hesitated to fill the void, skewing the biblical stories to reflect their own interests. Skeptical? Just ask yourself how Americans can believe that homosexuality is a major issue in the Bible and at the same time believe that the only relevant thing the Bible says about the poor is Jesus' (misinterpreted) statement that "the poor you will always have with you" (Matthew 26:11)? There are at most six passages in all of Scripture that could be interpreted to have direct bearing on the subject of homosexuality—and all of them are open to legitimate debate. Compare this with over *two thousand* passages that have to do with wealth and poverty and our responsibility to the poor. It is time to take our stories back—to proclaim them joyously and unapologetically. Storytelling must become just as important as advocacy work if Christian social justice is to have a chance at pushing deeply enough into the social system to matter.

A second implication is one proposed by Rabbi Michael Lerner, executive editor of *Tikkun* magazine and rabbi of the Beyt Tikkun community in Berkeley, California. Speaking before thirteen hundred individuals attending a conference on spiritual activism in July 2005, Rabbi Lerner made what he called a preliminary proposal for something all people of faith might work toward to change the system. He proposed that we add a Social Responsibility Amendment (SRA) to the Constitution. While Rabbi Lerner acknowledged that the details of such an amendment would need to be worked out extensively, he sketched its primary components to spark further thinking.

The SRA would require businesses with earnings of fifty million dollars per year to renew their business licenses every ten years. (In other words, this would not affect "mom and pop" shops.) As part of the renewal process, the businesses would have to prove to a jury of ordinary people that they have actively contributed to the well-being of the community. Was the company a good steward of the environment, for instance? Were its hiring practices just? Were its workers treated decently and fairly?

If the company could not demonstrate adequately that it had acted in socially responsible ways, it could lose its license. If it did act responsibly, its license would be renewed for another ten years.

Whether or not Rabbi Lerner's SRA ever becomes a serious proposal before the American public, what we need to find is a way all those "good people" in high places can actually do some good without themselves or their businesses being penalized. Socially responsible actions could be reasonably justified to stockholders in the name of protecting their investments. Further, a company's major competitors would face the same challenges. Something like the SRA would not merely bandage a broken system but could lead to reconstruction of the system itself—which is the point of the story of Amos. It would create a "new bottom line," as Rabbi Lerner calls it, where justice, decency, and fairness are valued as highly as (and not instead of) profitability.

If the SRA seems like an awfully big step to you, I encourage you to look for alternatives. It is doubtful that our system can be changed with minor course correctives. Any proposal that aims at healing the heart of the system is going to be large, with complicated implications that will take some time to digest properly. It is sad that no proposal of equal gravity seems to have been on the table in Amos' day. As Amos' story clearly demonstrates, when the system is broken, it is far riskier to do nothing at all than to act with boldness and make adjustments. It is not only the America of the present that is at stake; it is the America that we leave to our children.

seven

Preserving religious freedom and the church's ability to speak prophetically to government by resisting the commingling of church and state

AS CHRISTIANS, WE STRIVE to live as responsible citizens of our country, just as we seek to live as Christ's disciples. We celebrate the separation of church and state as much for the protection of the church and other faith communities as the state.

WE AFFIRM that the Path of Jesus is found where Christ's followers honor the role of the state in maintaining justice and peace, so far as human discernment and ability make possible. We affirm the separation of church and state, even as we endeavor to support the state in as far as Christian conscience allows.

WE CONFESS that we have moved away from this Path when we have confused the role of the state with that of the church. We have moved further from the Path when we have renounced the church's calling to speak prophetically to the state by suggesting that the church should or could take on the nature, tasks, and dignity that belong to the state, thus becoming itself an organ of the state.

I have no doubt that every new example will succeed,
as every past one has done, in showing that religion
and government will both exist in greater purity,
the less they are mixed together.

— JAMES MADISON, LETTER TO
EDWARD LIVINGSTON, JULY 10, 1822

Most Christians in the United States have little desire to im-
pose their faith on others. They may wish others would share
their convictions, and short of agreement, they will insist
on their right of conscience with respect to religion. Yet mainstream Christianity in America has traditionally supported the
separation of church and state. It is in the best interest of all to
do so. Moderate Christian conservatives and liberals both recognize, as James Madison did more than two centuries ago, that
"the same authority which can establish Christianity in exclusion of all other religions may establish, with the same ease, any
particular sect of Christians in exclusion of all other sects."[1]

As a minister of the United Church of Christ, my theological ancestors include the Congregationalist pilgrims who sailed
to America from England via Holland. Most Congregationalists
affirmed the separation of church and state primarily for the
protection of the church, not the state. They had experienced
first hand the religious persecution to which Madison alludes
when the Church of England used legislation to put an end to
alternative religious practices. While certain early colonists argued for instituting state sponsorship of Congregationalist faith
and practice as a hedge against further persecution of their reli-

gion, the fallacy of their reactionary stance was quickly evident. Congregationalist wisdom clearly headed toward protecting the church by *strengthening* the wall of separation, not taking it down.

In recent times, certain branches of Christianity have departed from this view. So-called Christian dominionists long for a day when Christians act as "the vice-regents of God" and "exercise godly dominion and influence over our neighborhoods, our schools, our government, our literature and arts, our sports arenas, our entertainment media, our news media, our scientific endeavors—in short, over every aspect and institution of human society."[2]

Yet most other Christians, liberal and conservative, are far more closely aligned in affirming the separation of church and state than people often realize. This resistance to commingling religious and political power comes not only from their common American heritage but also from their shared biblical tradition. Although there never was a strict separation between religion and politics in biblical times, the Bible consistently teaches that political authority, while necessary for the maintenance of order, works in the interest of neither God nor the people when religion uncritically embraces that authority. The relationship between religion and politics in the Bible is therefore marked by skepticism, challenge, and at times downright opposition.

In the Book of Judges, for instance, one finds a humorous parable of a group of trees who go out seeking someone to rule over them (Judges 9:8–15). They approach an olive tree, a fig tree, and a grape vine, asking each in turn to serve as king over them. All decline the proposition, explaining that they're too busy producing oil, figs, and wine to concern themselves with kingship. Then the trees approach a thorny bramble bush. The bramble, which produces nothing of value, is only too happy to rule over them. The parable, of course, takes a jab at political leaders, suggesting that if they had anything better to do, they wouldn't be governing the people.

The Book of Judges looks back, in fact, to a period in Israel's history when it was so skeptical about human political power that for about two hundred years, it chose to have no king at all. God alone was thought to be sovereign. Only when pressures from the surrounding nations gave rise to the need to conscript a military did Israel finally consent to allow a human leader to act as king. The day Israel first asked for a human ruler was no cause for celebration in the Bible. The prophet Samuel prayed to God, highly agitated over the people's desire for a king (1 Samuel 8:7–9). God is said to have answered Samuel this way:

Listen to the voice of the people in all that they say to you; for they have not rejected you, but they have rejected me from being king over them. Just as they have done to me, from the day I brought them up out of Egypt to this day, forsaking me and serving other gods, so also they are doing to you. Now, then, listen to their voice; only you shall solemnly warn them and show them the ways of the king who shall reign over them.

The paradox of God's approving the people's request for a human king combined with God's acknowledgment that their request constitutes a rejection of divine authority sets up a creative tension between religion and politics that remains throughout the majority of Israel's history. From this point on, prophetic leaders representing "true" religion are portrayed as standing against the state as well as advising and supporting it. Those who enjoy too cozy a relationship with the state are almost always portrayed as sell-outs and yes-men.

Take, for example, the story of the prophet Micaiah. In 1 Kings 22, Micaiah is summoned by Ahab, king of Israel, and Jehoshaphat, king of Judah, to deliver a "word from the Lord" concerning whether or not Israel and Judah should go to war against the king of Aram. Four hundred prophets, all in the employ of King Ahab, have already given the green light. They have enthusiastically confirmed Ahab's opinion that they should go to war, promising him easy success because the war is God's will. But Jehoshaphat isn't convinced that religious leaders so closely aligned with the king can be trusted. He asks Ahab if there is any other prophet who can inquire of the Lord. Reluctantly, Ahab summons Micaiah, an outsider to Ahab's court. Ahab grumbles, "I hate him, for he never prophesies anything favorable about me, but only disaster."

As the two kings await the arrival of Micaiah, the court prophets put on a grand show of support for the war effort. One leader takes a pair of iron ox horns, thrusting them in the air shouting, "With these you shall gore the Aramaeans until they are destroyed!" Others proclaim, "Go up . . . and triumph. The Lord will give it into the hand of the king!"

When the king's messenger reaches Micaiah, he encourages the prophet to confirm the words of the others, saying, "Look, the words of the prophets with one accord are favorable to the king; let your word be like the word of one of them, and speak favorably."

When Micaiah speaks against Ahab's warring ambition, he is promptly slapped in the face by Ahab's highest religious adviser and is sent to jail. In the end, however, Micaiah is vindicated. Ahab is killed in battle, and the armies of Israel and Judah are overrun by Aram.

This story illustrates a significant view in the Bible regarding the relationship between political and religious power. Whether it is Micaiah, the prophet Amos, or Elijah, Elisha, or Jeremiah, most authentic prophets in the Bible challenge more than confirm political leaders' authority. Like the four hundred prophets of Ahab's court, religious leaders who are too closely aligned with the state are portrayed as mere puppets who serve the interests of neither God nor the people.

To be sure, the biblical prophets are not always adversaries of the state. The prophet Nathan, for instance, served as a close friend and adviser to King David during his reign. However, this same prophet is responsible for one of the harshest criticisms of David in the entire Bible. Nathan can be more critical of David even than David's enemies![3]

In the New Testament, Jesus' relationship with the state is clearly not a comfortable one. Knowing this, a group of religious leaders try to trap Jesus into saying something that will land him jail. In front of a crowd that includes political leaders, they ask Jesus if it is appropriate to pay taxes to the emperor or not. "Aware of their malice," the Gospel of Matthew reports, Jesus asks them whose head and title is on a coin used to pay taxes. "The emperor's," they answer. Jesus replies, "Give therefore to the emperor the things that are the emperor's, and to God the things that are God's" (Matthew 22:16–22). It was Jesus' determination to serve no other master, giving what is God's to God rather than to the state (meaning his allegiance and devotion, his passion for love and justice, his hope and vision), which eventually led to Jesus' arrest and crucifixion as a common criminal.

Some Christians who argue for a closer relationship between church and state cite Paul's admonition in Romans 13:1–2: "Let every person be subject to the governing authorities; for there is no authority except from God, and those authorities that exist have been instituted by God. Therefore, whoever resists authority resists what God has appointed, and those who resist will incur judgment." Yet this passage must be interpreted in its scriptural context. It is preceded immediately by Paul's admonition, "Do not be overcome by evil, but overcome evil with good." In this context, then, Paul is counseling Christians who seek to resist political oppression not to commit evil acts against the government but to work only and always for the good, lest one destroy the good with the evil. Anyone who believes that Paul is advising Christians to embrace government uncritically needs to consider how many times Paul went to prison for his beliefs and the fact that Paul was later executed by the very government about which he writes in Romans 13.

WALKING THE TALK

As tempting as it has been at times for American Christians to seek state support for church values, both American history and biblical tradition have served as a helpful corrective, making it clear that short-term gains lead to long-term problems. A government that smiles one day on one form of religion may just as easily frown on it the next. If one gives to the emperor what properly belongs to God, whether in the name of patriotism or even in the name of Jesus, one has clearly left the stream of American patriotic tradition and of Jewish and Christian biblical tradition.

One area where the wall of separation is particularly poignant in American life today is the issue of same-sex marriage. The vast majority of arguments against same-sex marriage are religiously based. Yet in traditionally mainline Christian denominations—including Presbyterian, Methodist, Episcopal, Disciples of Christ, Lutheran, and United Church of Christ—significant arguments are being advanced on biblical and theological grounds in support of same-sex marriage and gay and lesbian equality in general. In fact, the United Church of Christ overwhelmingly passed a resolution in support of same-sex marriage at its general synod in 2005, and the Episcopal Church has confirmed an openly gay bishop. These decisions remain controversial, but whether one is for or against same-sex marriage, those who affirm the separation of church and state would do well to consider what is at stake when seeking to pass legislation beyond the church that establishes one religious perspective over that of another.

Not only would a ban on same-sex marriage violate the First Amendment to the Constitution, which states that "Congress shall make no law respecting the establishment of religion, or prohibiting the free exercise thereof," but it violates an important principle of the Bible. Whereas homosexuality is a minor issue in the Bible, Scripture has much to say about the problems resulting from creating too cozy a relationship between religious and political authority.

The bottom line is, when we give the emperor what properly belongs to God, we must bear in mind that the emperor will always seek to use his enhanced power to *play* God. The wall of separation between church and state protects the church more than it does the state. Thus mainstream American Christians have always found it far better to err on the side of safeguarding religious freedom than to err on the side of empowering the emperor.

eight

Walking humbly with God, acknowledging our own shortcomings while honestly seeking to understand and call forth the best in others, including those who consider us their enemies

AS CHRISTIANS, WE RECOGNIZE that we are misfits both with respect to God's Realm and the world. We are misfits with respect to God's Realm in that we rarely live up to the principles and ideals we espouse. We are misfits with respect to the world in that the ideals for which we strive frequently do not conform to the ways of the world.

WE AFFIRM that the Path of Jesus is found where Christ's followers love those who consider them their enemies as much as they love themselves, striving humbly to embody the "fruits of the Spirit": love, joy, peace, patience, kindness, generosity, faithfulness, gentleness, and self-control.

WE CONFESS that we have moved away from this Path when we have promoted a notion that people of faith are morally or ethically superior to those without faith. Further, we have moved away when we have supported any cause, no matter how just or righteous, without reflecting the "fruits of the Spirit" toward all.

Love your enemy—it will scare the hell out of them.

—Attributed to Mark Twain

Have you ever noticed that Christians who tend to be most insistent about the need for tolerance, unconditional love, and open-mindedness are often some of the most closed-minded, intolerant, and unloving people? They are equaled in vitriol and prejudice only by Christians who stand against tolerance as a "concession to evil," who preach salvation only for the "righteous" (read "self-righteous"), and believe there is no need to be open-minded when one is right to begin with.

How do people supposedly following the same teachings become so polarized? As different as they are, the extreme Right and Left within Christianity frequently seem quite similar. Both sides may believe they are standing up for Jesus or for love and justice, but on a deeper level, they are united by a fear and loathing of their enemies that often trumps the good they believe they represent. In my wanderings on both sides of the religious divide, I have found absolutely unanimous agreement, in theory, with Jesus' command to love our neighbors as we love ourselves. I've even found unanimous agreement with his command to "love your enemies, do good to those who hate you, bless those who curse you, pray for those who abuse you" (Luke 6:27–28). Yet everyone—myself included—seems to struggle with this concept.

I remember vividly as a young teenager watching an old cowboy movie where a group of outlaws pull up on horseback to a settler family's home and demand that the settlers turn over one of their sons against whom the outlaws have a grudge. The father of the house confronts the outlaws by holding up a cross affixed to a chain around his neck. He demands that the outlaws leave "in Jesus' name," apparently acting on faith in Jesus' assurance that "whatsoever you ask of the Father in my name will be given to you" (John 16:23). The outlaws don't budge. Then, as the man begins reciting the Lord's Prayer, the outlaw leader shoots him dead.

To me, this scene served as a vivid illustration that there is theory and then there is practice. There are ideals and there is the "real" world. Most of us, I believe, truly want to practice Jesus' ideal of loving our neighbor as ourselves *so long as our neighbor is doing it as well*. We stumble when we realize that if we strongly commit to loving our neighbor while our neighbor is actively working against our own or others' well-being, we or those we love are not going to be long for this world. When conflict develops, we affirm Jesus' command in principle even as it fails to make a difference in our practice.

Was Jesus naive when he said that loving our neighbor as we love ourselves is one of the two greatest commandments? Was he simply an idealistic dreamer when he insisted that this principle applies even to our enemies? Perhaps Jesus simply lived in a kinder, gentler time. Maybe if he'd realized the kinds of threats we'd be up against in the modern world, he'd have changed his tune.

Jesus is not the only one to teach these principles. They appear in one form or another in all the major world religions. In 500 B.C.E., for instance, Confucius taught his followers the habit of *shu*, or "likening to oneself." "Do not do to others as you would not have done unto you," he advised. The Buddha taught his followers to practice the Immeasurables, meditation exercises in which one practices sending out thoughts of compassion, benevolence, and sympathy to every single creature on earth. The great Rabbi Hillel, an immediate predecessor of Jesus, taught, "That which is hateful to you, do not do to your neighbor. That is the Torah; the rest is commentary; go and learn it!"

If Jesus was naive or unrealistic in his insistence on loving our neighbor as we love ourselves, then so were the founders of all the great world religions. There are good reasons, however, why we may consider their advice as more realistic and practical than is commonly supposed.

For instance, the future of the world is at stake. We presently have the capacity literally to wipe ourselves off the face of the planet. Americans—and several other nations—possess the infamous weapons of mass destruction we were looking so hard to find in Iraq. Can we afford to allow fear and hatred to build between nations that have such weapons? Further, as events of recent years have illustrated all too well in our own country, it does not take much more than a little fertilizer, a few handguns, or control of an airplane cockpit to unleash unspeakable evil. Indeed, since the beginning of human history, it has never been easier than it is now to convert personal hatred into mass destruction. Can we assume that our enemies will learn to love us if we do not find ways to extend love to them? If not, will we really be safer simply by building up our mechanisms to thwart their attempts to harm us?

Though loving our neighbor puts us at distinct risk if our neighbor does not love us back, is it really any less risky *not* to love our neighbor? Lives can and certainly will be lost if we take seriously Jesus' command to "bless those who curse you" and to "turn the other cheek" when struck, but can it reasonably be assumed that fewer lives will be lost by "doing unto others as they would do unto us"? When push comes to shove, our pushing and shoving blinds us to more peaceful and creative alternatives. And sadly, no matter how righteous we believe our cause to be and no matter how egregious the actions of our neighbors, the trajectory of hatred always leads to one place: becoming the very thing we hate.

Consider the responses to Hurricane Katrina in 2005. Immediately after the hurricane struck the Gulf Coast, public compassion for the hurricane's victims surged, particularly for the residents of New Orleans. Yet even as many were digging deep to send money, clothing, and supplies and opening their homes to refugees, others were rushing to use the tragedy as proof of the insidiousness of their enemies. The hurricane was blamed on American imperialists,[1] on abortion providers,[2] on Republicans,[3] on Democrats,[4] on homosexuals,[5] and even on the Israeli government.[6]

Could all these groups be responsible for the hurricane or the suffering that occurred in its wake? Of course not. We live in a time when it is getting increasingly dangerous to hate our enemy. Failing to love our neighbor—even when that neighbor is actively working against our well-being—is rapidly becoming a recipe for mass destruction and unimaginable hardship.

This does not mean that we should take up an extremist position of another kind and lay down every weapon we have or remain passive in the face of what we perceive as evil. To do nothing in the face of evil is to allow evil free rein. Jesus himself insisted that we are to be "wise as serpents and innocent as doves" (Matthew 10:16) even as he commanded us to love our enemies. Are these principles contradictory, or are we just not seeing the bigger picture?

Once again, it is often easier to see that bigger picture by turning to a smaller one. When I was first learning to drive, I remember gunning my way through a light that had changed from green to yellow. My father, sitting beside me, said, "You should've stopped."

"But Dad," I countered, "the light was yellow the whole way through!"

He then said something that rankled me terribly at the time. "Eric, always remember: 'Johnny was right. Dead right. But now he's as dead as he was right.'"

Through the years, this expression has echoed in my mind more times than I can count, in response to far more situations than passing through intersections. No matter how right or righteous we may believe our cause to be, we can destroy ourselves just as easily as we can save ourselves, particularly when we encounter dangerous intersections in life. If we do not learn to see the humanity in our neighbors even as we struggle with them over issues of justice and righteousness, we will surely lose the very things we hold most dear. If we cannot perceive that at base we are more the same than different, we will not gain what we seek most urgently.

Jesus' call to love our neighbor as we love ourselves serves as a critical reminder that our neighbor is not as much of a stranger as we may suppose. In an interview in *Sun* magazine, author David Duncan states succinctly the astonishing effect that overcoming the strangeness of our neighbor has on our actions:

> Christ's words "Love thy neighbor as thyself" . . . demand an arduous imaginative act. These peculiar words order me, as I look at you, to imagine that I am seeing not you but me, and then to treat this imaginative me, alias you, as if you *are* me. And for how long? Till the day I die! Christ orders those who are serious about him to commit this "my neighbor is me" fiction until they forget, for good and all, which of the two "me's" to cheat in a business deal or punch in a fight or abandon in a crisis or shoot in a war.[7]

Often dialogues between two opposing sides break down because there is more than one right answer and neither side can bring itself to acknowledge the other side's point. If both sides would seek first to acknowledge the right answers that their neighbors have (and both sides will have some), then both sides can be more open to finding an answer, or a set of answers, that transcends any of their original answers. There is more often than not a third way between two opposing points of view.

Along the way in this process of finding a third way, it's OK to make mistakes. That might sound just fine, but when tensions run high, I find myself like Peter asking Jesus, "Just how many times are we to forgive the mistakes of others?" Peter suggests, "As many as seven times?" to which Jesus responds, "Not seven but seventy times seven" (Matthew 18:21–22). Sometimes I have a hard time forgiving others for their mistakes (or forgiving myself for my own) because I don't think mistakes should be made to begin with. But in many situations, mistakes—even big ones—are part of the natural process of living a creative life. In my own work at Scottsdale Congregational United Church of Christ, I have found this simple idea to be essential, and not simply for facing opposition from others. For example, I work with a worship team for three hours each week. In the six years we've been designing worship, we normally find we need to blow through ten bad ideas for every good one we keep. Often we look back and realize that if we hadn't taken one of the bad ideas seriously, we never would have been led to the good one. In this sense, there truly are no bad ideas.

I have found this principle to apply every bit as much to my personal life. When it comes to encountering opposition from others, the assurance that it's OK to make mistakes cuts two ways. First, I realize that it's OK if I make mistakes in my encounter with my neighbor. It's also OK if I'm proved wrong. This makes me less defensive. Second, I realize that it's OK for my neighbor to be wrong too. In fact, in our life paths, both my neighbor and I probably need to be absolutely convinced of ten wrong things for every one thing we discover that's truly transcendent. This is a humbling fact of life but a true one—which is probably why God believes so strongly in grace and forgiveness.

When we learn to bring our common humanity to the table in our personal struggles with others, even as we bring our critiques, we are in a vastly better position to negotiate by using these same dynamics at the community level (including the national and international levels). Perhaps this is why Jesus focused so strongly on the individual lives of his followers—not because he was disinterested in the larger picture but because we don't have much of a chance at living creatively on a large scale until we've learned a few things about living this way in our everyday lives. If we truly learn to love our neighbor as we love ourselves, there is much reason to hope both for our personal lives and for our planet. As Jesus promises, for those who do so, "your reward will be great, and you will be children of the Most High; for [God] is kind to the ungrateful and the wicked" (Luke 6:35).

WALKING THE TALK

One of the mistakes people often make when sincerely trying to love those with whom they struggle is that they assume that no one must ever get angry or upset. Given the opportunity to meet their opposition face to face, they feel guilty if the encounter doesn't end in group hugs and a round of "Kumbaya." This often leads to the unspoken assumption that there are certain things that should not be said. While it is certainly appropriate—even advisable—to set the parameters of respectful dialogue, it is equally important to keep the conversation real. When no one is fully committed to the effort, it ends up feeling like a charade. Honest communication suffers. Another common mistake is entering into an encounter believing that if one just makes the right arguments or speaks intelligently enough, the opposition will immediately come around and will be thankful for being set straight. The reality is that even if you are able to win someone over, the other person will not necessarily thank you for it! Jesus was not crucified by those who thought his points were irrelevant.

It is important to be realistic in your expectations. In fact, it is best to be very intentional and clear that you are not seeking to "convert" the other person. Rather, you are seeking to listen. Your goal is to listen deeply enough that you can start to see how, if you believed all the same things, you could hold the same point of view. It could well be that after seeing things the way the other person does, you will see the error of your own ways. In any case, it is unlikely that you will be able to offer your point of view in the way it needs to be expressed until you have listened intently to the other person. If you do this well, the other person will likely walk away from the encounter more open to your point of view than when you started. Not convinced, perhaps, but more open than before.

nine

Basing our lives on the faith that in Christ all things are made new and that we, and all people, are loved beyond our wildest imagination—for eternity

AS CHRISTIANS, WE BEAR WITNESS TO, and nurture faith in, all persons who are hungry for or open to the revelation, love, and salvation of God in Christ. We do not seek to evangelize those who have no desire to explore the Christian Path. We trust, rather, that God's love, grace, and invitation have been and will be revealed in other paths, witnesses, and times.

WE AFFIRM that the Path of Jesus is found where Christ's followers are continually discovering and rediscovering that they—and all people—are loved beyond their wildest imagination, and they determine to live their lives according to this discovery. We find in this discovery and surrender the very essence of salvation, which is a process, not an end point, within an eternal journey.

WE CONFESS that we have moved away from this Path whenever we have denied God's love for all people or have denied the effectiveness of God's eternal will that all be saved. We have moved further from Christ's Path when we have not actively born witness to God's love and grace with those who seek it.

Earth's crammed with heaven.
And every common bush aflame with God.
But only he who sees takes off his shoes.
The rest sit round it and pluck blackberries.
— Elizabeth Barrett Browning (1806–1861)

A couple of years ago, two biblical scholars who had each written books on Jesus were featured on a talk show on National Public Radio. One scholar came from the more conservative end of the theological spectrum; the other, from the liberal end. When the host took calls from listeners, the first was from a man around thirty-five years old whose voice shook with anxiety as he proceeded to ask a question that had nothing to do with their books or their differing views of Jesus. The man was asking these two acclaimed biblical scholars about salvation. He had not been to church in many years, but recently he had started attending with his young daughter.

All was well and good . . . at least until his daughter started telling him what she was learning in Sunday school. Yes, she learned about how God loves us. But she was also learning that unless she believed a certain way, she and anyone like her would be thrown into a lake of fire for eternity.

The slight quiver in this man's voice reflected the inner pain behind his question: "Am I *way off base* here? I believe God *loves* us. Am I way off base to believe that God would not throw someone to be tortured in hell for eternity?"

You could pick up on the hesitation in the scholars' voices as they began to make their responses, each in turn. You could feel them wondering, "How am I going to phrase this without triggering ten thousand pieces of hate mail tomorrow?" Interestingly, even though they held very different views of Jesus, both came out in a similar direction. They emphasized that Jesus had precious little to say about the afterlife. Jesus focused like a laser on this-world realities. Therefore, any Christian theology that grounds itself in a definitive concept of the afterlife is based on something very different from what Jesus based his teachings on.

The scholars both answered the caller as if he were posing an academic question. But he was really asking, "Will my child and I be tortured for eternity if we don't come to believe as our church does?" He also seemed to be asking, "Is my faith in a loving God all in vain?" So much more could have been said.

Most people in traditionally mainline churches don't talk much about souls burning in hell for eternity. It doesn't fit well with our reading of Scripture or Christian tradition. Yet although neither the Bible nor the earliest Christian traditions support a notion of hell as popularly conceived, both Scripture and nearly two thousand years of Christian tradition assert that *Jesus saves*—that somehow our faith in Christ saves us *from* something and *for* something. What could that be?

In the story of a tax collector named Zacchaeus in Luke 19, Jesus is walking through Jericho on his way to Jerusalem. The crowd accompanying him through the city is so large that Zacchaeus climbs up in a tree to get a good view. You can imagine what the crowds are telling Jesus when Zacchaeus is spotted in the tree.

"There's that lousy traitor Zacchaeus! Why don't you preach a 'word from the Lord' to him, Jesus? He's a fellow Jew, for goodness sake, yet he's become rich by participating in the Roman looting of our land. Imagine—a *Jew* collecting ungodly taxes from his own people!"

Seeing Jesus and the crowd advancing toward him, Zacchaeus starts thinking that this isn't what he bargained for. All he wanted to do was inconspicuously get a glimpse of Jesus from a safe distance. Now there's no escape! What will this revolutionary character say? Will he call him a thief and a traitor? Will he command them to grab a noose for a lynching?

When Jesus draws near, he calls to Zacchaeus, saying, "Zacchaeus, hurry and come down, for I must stay at your house today." The crowd is outraged, but Zacchaeus climbs down from the tree.

Obviously relieved and overwhelmed with Jesus' public and highly controversial expression of welcome, Zacchaeus stands before the angry mob and announces, "Look, half of my possessions, Lord, I will give to the poor; and if I have defrauded anyone of anything, I will pay back four times as much." In response, Jesus says, "Today, *salvation* has come to this house."

When does salvation come for Zacchaeus? Jesus does not say, "*When you die* salvation *will come* to your house"; he says, "*Today* salvation *has come* . . ." Salvation in this instance means that radical grace has changed Zacchaeus' heart, inspiring him to live by a different set of priorities. His change of heart manifests itself concretely in an act of justice, promising to restore fourfold what he has taken unjustly from the community. It also manifests itself in astonishing generosity toward the poor. Further, salvation likely implies a degree of reconciliation with the community as Zacchaeus acts with justice and generosity. We miss the point if we assume that Jesus is announcing something good that will happen to Zacchaeus once he dies. Zacchaeus is saved *from* greed, injustice, and living as an outcast and *for* generosity, honesty, fairness, and reconciliation with his enemies. His community also benefits profoundly from Zacchaeus' change of heart.

Similar this-world benefits of salvation are depicted time after time in the Gospels. The benefits are sometimes forgiveness and reconciliation (as in Luke 7, where Jesus announces to an unnamed woman, "Your faith has saved you"); physical rescue, as in the case of the disciples caught in a storm (Matthew 8:24–27); or healing, as in the case of the woman with a hemorrhage (Matthew 9; Mark 5; Luke 8) or a blind man receiving sight (Luke 18:35–43). In these cases and many more, when Jesus announces that a person is "saved," the import of the statement has to do primarily with physical or spiritual transformation in this world. Jesus' concept of salvation appears fully in line with that of his Hebrew ancestors. This is not to say that Jesus or the Hebrews were only ever interested in salvation in this life as opposed to the next, but this is such a strong and consistent emphasis that it is questionable whether one can even begin to understand salvation in the next life before one grasps its importance in this one.

One of my favorite stories that gets to the essence of Jesus' view of salvation was written comparatively recently, by Victor

Hugo in his nineteenth-century novel *Les Misérables*, on which the Broadway musical is based.

The central character, Jean Valjean, has just been released on probation from prison after having served nineteen years at hard labor. As part of his probation, he is required to show his criminal record to anyone with whom he comes into contact, whether he's seeking lodging for the night or employment.

Valjean quickly discovers that showing his probation papers makes him an outcast. Village after village rejects him, refusing him lodging, food, and employment.

Late one night, on the brink of starvation and insanity, Valjean seeks help at the home of a humble priest. Out of habit, Valjean reaches into his back pocket and produces his probation papers, waiting for the priest's stern rebuke and dismissal. Instead, the priest graciously invites Valjean to join him to dine and stay the night. The priest proceeds to treat Valjean as if he is in the company of Jesus Christ himself. He sets out his best silver tableware for Valjean. He offers Valjean the finest food from his larder.

Early in the morning, when Valjean awakens in the priest's guest room, he is so used to being a reject and a convict that he stuffs his knapsack with the silver place settings used at the dinner table the night before and flees.

Valjean does not even make it to the other side of town before he is caught with the damning probation papers and a knapsack crammed with expensive silverware. Valjean denies the theft, claiming that the priest gave him the items.

Three policemen drag Valjean to the priest's house to return the silver and take him back to prison. Yet when they arrive and escort Valjean inside, the priest looks him in the eye and exclaims, "Ah! Here you are! I am glad to see you. Well, but how is this? I gave you the candlesticks too, which are of silver like the rest, and for which you can certainly get two hundred francs. Why did you not carry them away with your forks and spoons?"

The police are dumfounded. "Monseigneur," the senior officer stammers, "so what this man said is true then? We came across him. He was walking like a man who is running away. We stopped him to look into the matter. He had this silver—"

"And he told you," interposes the priest with a smile, "that it had been given to him by a kind old fellow of a priest with whom he had passed the night? I see how the matter stands. And you have brought him back here? It is a mistake."

Valjean has never experienced God's grace like this before, mediated through the clever lie of a forgiving priest. When he reaches out and grasps the candlesticks, it is as if the priest has reached down deep into his soul, through the muck and mire, and drawn up gold—or in this case, purest silver. Valjean has experienced the kind of grace and love for which people readily give up their lives in order to carry even a small portion in their heart.

From this point on, Valjean lives not simply as an honest man but as a courageous man who, through deep personal sacrifice, continually reaches into the souls of others and brings up gold.

To define succinctly what salvation means in *Les Misérables* and in the Gospels, one could say that salvation is *discovering that we are loved beyond our wildest imagination and then determining to live our lives according to this discovery.*

In answer to the man's implied question on the radio about whether he and his daughter can expect God to throw them into hell for eternity if they do not come to believe as their church believes, I would ask a simple question: "What do you suppose the priest in *Les Misérables* would do if he were God? Now what do you suppose *Jesus* would do?"

WALKING THE TALK

A number of writers in the Bible reflect on how God, or God in Christ, acts as Savior in this life and draw implications for how God acts toward us in the next. Although the Bible does not speak with a single voice regarding these implications, it is curious to note that many of the voices reflect some notion of salvation for all people. They may not assume that salvation happens instantaneously after a person dies—Paul, for instance, speaks of multiple levels of heaven (see 2 Corinthians 12:1–4)—but they give voice to a notion that God's grace is far greater than most people expect. Given that these passages are rarely cited by those who feel that our eternal state rests on some form of perfect belief in this life, I quote several passages to read and reflect on. Taken as a whole, they point to a God who looks a lot like, well, Jesus!

All the ends of the earth shall remember and turn to the LORD; and *all the families of the nations* shall worship before him. For dominion belongs to the LORD, and *he rules over the nations.* To him, indeed, shall *all who sleep in the earth* bow down; before him shall bow *all who go down to the dust,* and I shall live for him. Posterity will serve him; future generations will be told about the Lord, and proclaim his deliverance to a people yet unborn, saying that he has done it. (Psalm 22:27–31)

Where can I go from your spirit? Or where can I flee from your presence? If I ascend to heaven, you are there; *if I make my bed in Sheol* [the underworld], *you are there.* If I take the wings of the morning and settle at the farthest limits of the sea, even there your hand shall lead me, and your right hand shall hold me fast. If I say, "Surely the darkness shall cover me, and the light around me become night," even the darkness is not dark to you; the night is as bright as the day, for darkness is as light to you. (Psalm 139:7–12)

When they came to the place that is called The Skull, they crucified Jesus there with the criminals, one on his right and one on his left. Then Jesus said, *"Father, forgive them; for they do not know what they are doing."* (Luke 23:33–34)[1]

The next day [John the Baptist] saw Jesus coming toward him and declared, "Here is the Lamb of God *who takes away the sin of the world!"* (John 1:29)

For God so loved the world that he gave his only Son, so that everyone who believes in him may not perish but may have eternal life. Indeed, *God did not send the Son into the world to condemn the world, but in order that the world might be saved* through him. (John 3:16–17)[2]

Therefore just as one man's trespass led to condemnation for all, so one man's act of righteousness leads to *justification and life for all*. For just as by the one man's disobedience the many were made sinners, so by the one man's obedience *the many will be made righteous*. (Romans 5:18–19)

For I am convinced that neither death, nor life, nor angels, nor rulers, nor things present, nor things to come, nor powers, nor height, nor depth, *nor anything else in all creation, will be able to separate us from the love of God in Christ Jesus our Lord.* (Romans 8:38–9:1)

For since death came through a human being, the resurrection of the dead has also come through a human being; *for as all die in Adam, so all will be made alive in Christ.* (1 Corinthians 15:21–22)

In Christ God was reconciling the world to himself, not counting their trespasses against them, and entrusting the message of reconciliation to us. (2 Corinthians 5:19)

In him we have redemption through his blood, the forgiveness of our trespasses, according to the riches of his grace that he lavished on us. With all wisdom and insight he has made known to us the mystery of his will, according to his good pleasure that he set forth in Christ, as a plan for the fullness of time, *to gather up all things in him, things in heaven and things on earth.* (Ephesians 1:7–10)

For in him all the fullness of God was pleased to dwell, and through him *God was pleased to reconcile to himself all things, whether on earth or in heaven,* by making peace through the blood of his cross. (Colossians 1:19–20)

This is right and is acceptable in the sight of God our Savior, *who desires everyone to be saved* and to come to the knowledge of the truth. For there is one God; there is also one mediator between God and humankind, Christ Jesus, himself human, *who gave himself a ransom for all*—this was attested at the right time. (1 Timothy 2:3–6)

For Christ *also suffered for sins once for all, the righteous for the unrighteous,* in order to bring you to God. He was put to death in the flesh, but made alive in the spirit, in which also *he went and made a proclamation to the spirits in prison* [i.e., the underworld]. (1 Peter 3:18–19)

But do not ignore this one fact, beloved, that with the Lord one day is like a thousand years, and a thousand years are like one day. *The Lord is not slow about his promise, as some think of slowness, but is patient with you, not wanting any to perish, but all to come to repentance.* (2 Peter 3:8–9)

After this I looked, and there was *a great multitude that no one could count, from every nation, from all tribes and peoples and languages,* standing before the throne and before the Lamb, robed in white, with palm branches in their hands. They cried out in a loud voice, saying, "Salvation belongs to our God who is seated on the throne, and to the Lamb!" (Revelation 7:9–10)

ten

Claiming the sacredness of both our minds and our hearts and recognizing that faith and science, doubt and belief serve the pursuit of truth

As Christians, we seek to develop intellectually as sincerely as we seek emotional development. We further seek to clarify that the truths contained in Scripture are not conveyed primarily through scientific revelations but through wisdom that may be gleaned in story and song, symbol and parable.

We affirm that the Path of Jesus is found where Christ's followers value the pursuit of wisdom, which is found at the intersection of head and heart, where God seeks relationship with the human soul.

We confess that we have moved away from this Path when we have denied either the role of the mind or that of the heart in the seeking of wisdom. Further, we have moved off the Path when we have denigrated the role of doubt or pursuit of scientific knowledge as if they were enemies rather than allies of faith.

It's not that we fear the unknown. You cannot fear something
that you do not know. Nobody is afraid of the unknown.
What you really fear is the loss of the known.
—ANTHONY DE MELLO, *Awareness*

The root word for both *mind* and *heart* in biblical Hebrew is the
same (*leb*). In biblical Greek, the word for *heart* (*kardia*) often
stands for *mind* as well. These simple facts, embedded in the
very roots of biblical language, suggest that engaging both mind
and heart is essential in the biblical faith. In our day, rich and
lively conversions over the integration of faith and science,
doubt, emotion, and belief are not only warranted from a biblical perspective but are also an essential part of a mature Christian faith. Such conversations, held between people honestly
seeking greater understanding, are normally fruitful even when
the conversation partners disagree over the implications of the
discussions.

Yet judging from the debates that rage over the relationship
between Christian faith and scientific endeavor, it seems as
though the human mind and heart are located at polar ex-
tremes of the human soul. Nowhere is this more apparent than
in the debates that have spanned nearly a century regarding the
creation of the earth and cosmos.

Some Christians, often known as "creationists," follow a literal reading of the first three chapters of Genesis, believing that
the universe was created in six literal days; the earth is mere
thousands of years old, not billions; no animals were originally

carnivores; the earth was created before the stars; plants were created before the sun; and humanity was present from the very beginning of things rather than arriving at a relatively recent point (or stretch of evolutionary time) in the earth's history.

Other Christians, following advancements in modern science as well as in literary theory and historical research regarding Scripture, hold sharply contrasting beliefs. They read the Creation stories for the spiritual truths they contain, not the historical claims. This approach, they point out, is more in keeping with how the stories were read in ancient times. Thus in their view, there is no essential contradiction between biblical faith and modern science.

Sadly, many debates among Christians of differing views have been held not in churches but rather in public school systems, government legislative bodies, and state and federal courtrooms. Therefore, almost from the start, discussions have been highly politicized, with opposing groups rarely seeking to engage one another in any other way than defensively or offensively.

In such a combative context, it looks as though we are locked into a struggle between competing interests that will continue to generate more heat than light, whose effects will be suffered more acutely by our children than ourselves. Is it possible that the Christian community can play a more productive role in this conflict? If so, the Christian community itself will have to change. We cannot keep engaging in the same old debates expecting different results. Those who locate themselves within the emerging Christian faith have an opportunity to put that faith into practice by working to shed more light in a deadlocked century-old discussion.

Think what would it be like if Christians could hold an authentic conversation like the one that follows.

Janet and Linda have been good friends since college days at Arizona State University twenty years ago. After graduation, Janet moved to Topeka, Kansas, and Linda remained in Phoenix. The two women are educated, intelligent, upper-middle-class professionals who share a number of interests. On a couple of occasions over the past twenty years, their families have joined together for vacations. Both Linda and Janet enjoy bird watching and hiking, and both actively volunteer in their communities. They are deeply involved in their respective churches.

Between business travel and vacations, Linda and Janet have been fortunate enough to see each other once every year or two since college. When they get together, they excitedly talk about seemingly every subject under the sun—except one. Even though they are both people of faith, they have learned to steer clear of religion. Whenever the subject has come up in the past, the conversation has either ended abruptly or ended in tears. At one point, they each made the unspoken decision to avoid the subject of faith to preserve their friendship.

Last year things changed, however. When Janet passed through Phoenix on a business trip, they met at a local coffeehouse. Both were troubled by a highly publicized debate on the Kansas State School Board over whether to include information regarding creationism and intelligent design along with evolution in science classes. Both knew that the other would be upset, for different reasons. Yet both instinctively decided to delicately raise the subject over coffee that morning in the hopes that as friends, they could finally get to the bottom of a sticking point in their relationship over the years.

Linda began by asking "innocently" how Janet felt the controversy was playing out in Kansas.

Knowing full well the import of Linda's question, Janet nevertheless decided to risk telling Linda exactly how she really felt.

"I just don't understand what the big deal is over teaching biblical truths to our children. It seems that every time people of faith try to open their mouths about anything these days, we come under attack. We live in a country that supposedly honors freedom of speech, but that seems to mean freedom to say anything you like other than speak God's Word. The Bible clearly says that God created the heavens and the earth in six days. People of faith don't want secular humanism passed off as science in school."

Linda felt her temper rising. She was offended that Janet would assume that only creationists are "people of faith." She wanted to tell Janet that she would no more want her children taught that God created the world in six days than that the moon was made of cheese. But something told her to bite her tongue. If Janet believed in a literal reading of Genesis, it was not because she was simple-minded. She decided to explore further.

"Do you believe it's possible to believe in both God and evolution?"

Janet hesitated a split second and then replied, "I know that some Christians think that it doesn't matter if the earth is a thousand years old or billions, but this isn't a trivial point at all. The Bible is God's Word. If you can't trust Genesis to be literally true, then how can you trust the rest of the Bible?

"Do you remember Marla Hedford?" Janet continued. "She and her husband scrimped and saved for years to send their son Thomas to a Christian college, thinking he'd be educated in the historic, biblical truths. But they're not even teaching the Bible as God's Word in Bible colleges these days. Marla called me a couple of months ago in tears saying that Thomas didn't believe the Bible anymore. She said he wasn't sure if he was even a Christian. That's his salvation we're talking about! He may lose his salvation at a *Christian* college! This is what happens when people decide there's something 'cooler' or more 'socially acceptable' than living by the plain, simple truths of Scripture. I think that's why Genesis is the focal point of Satan's attacks right now. He knows it will lead people away from their salvation."

"Our salvation hinges on what we believe about Genesis?"

"You don't understand, Linda," Janet replied anxiously. "There *is* a connection. But it's not as simple as losing faith in Genesis and automatically losing salvation. Genesis teaches that God created a perfect world. Adam and Eve lived in paradise. There was no death or judgment because there was no sin. Then, the Bible says, Adam and Eve turned their backs on God by eating forbidden fruit. At that moment, sin entered the world. And with sin came death. Humanity came under God's judgment and curse.

"So," Janet continued, "if the evolutionists are right, or even the so-called intelligent design people, then death was in the world *before* Adam and Eve's sin, for millions of years. This would mean that God created death; that death isn't punishment for sin but actually part of God's design."

"What would be wrong with that?"

"If God intended for us to die from the beginning," Janet answered, "then God isn't a God of love. God's a sadist. If 'survival of the fittest' is God's law and trillions of innocent animals and human beings have to suffer horrifying fates because of it, how could God be compassionate?"

"I've never understood it this way, Janet." Linda responded. Janet's views were completely different from her own, but instead of choosing to rebut them, she asked to hear more. "What does this have to do with salvation?"

"This is *all about* salvation," Janet replied. "Death is the result of God's *judgment on sin*, not part of God's plan. As long as there's death in the world, all of Creation is under the judgment. There's no way to be saved. But the Good News of the Gospel is that Jesus Christ came as the first sinless soul since Adam. As God's son, he was the only one born into the world since Adam without the guilt of sin or judgment. By dying innocently on the cross, Jesus took the judgment that should rightfully be ours upon himself. By rising from the dead, he conquered death and sin forever! From that day until now, salvation has been possible for anyone who believes in Jesus as Lord and Savior."

"So," Linda replied slowly to make sure she was understanding everything, "you're saying that if evolutionary theory is correct, then Jesus' death on the cross is meaningless. And if death isn't connected to sin, then resurrection isn't connected to the overcoming of sin."

"Exactly," said Janet. "Which means we're stuck in our sins. There's no salvation, only judgment. To me that makes God look a lot like Satan."

"Wow," exclaimed Linda. "I had no idea creationism was so connected to so many other beliefs. It sounds like you don't agree with the theory of intelligent design then either, since death would have been part of the world before Adam and Eve too."

"You got it," said Linda. "It really makes me angry that the news media are painting these intelligent design people as creationists who are just trying to cover up their beliefs. It shows that they haven't even taken the time to understand our views. What they don't realize is that ID is just as big a threat to the Gospels as out-and-out evolutionary theory. In fact, it's worse. It's like trying to deny the Gospels but sugar-coating it with a lot of God talk."

"I appreciate what you've told me," Linda said, "even though I disagree with your basic premises. I have to confess that I hadn't taken the time to understand them either. I know a little more now why there's so much emotion behind the creation versus evolution debate. I used to think the differences could be resolved with more scientific evidence one way or another, but it looks like theology and biblical interpretation are more of an issue than science. You understand salvation to be tied to the story, and others don't."

At this point, Janet was feeling a bit guilty that she'd been doing all the talking. "So what's your view? How can you call yourself a Christian and not believe that Jesus is your Savior?"

"I *do* believe Jesus is my Savior, and I have to confess that it hurts me when I hear people suggest that I can't possibly be a 'true believer' or believe in Jesus as my Savior if I think the world was created in more than six days."

"I'm sorry if I contributed to that," said Janet. "I know you're sincere about your faith. You took the time to listen to me explain my views, so now I'm all ears. How can you reconcile your beliefs against God's Word in the Bible?"

"Personally, I've never found that doubting certain claims in the Bible sets me against finding God's Word in it. In my experience, I've grown to know and love Scripture more since I realized that I don't have to take it all literally. Did you know, for instance, that there isn't just one Creation story in Genesis but two?"

"What do you mean?" asked Janet.

"I attended a Bible study on Genesis at my church last fall, and our pastor, who studied Hebrew in seminary, showed us all kinds of differences in language and style between the first chapter and the next. She said that most mainstream biblical scholars have known for the last century that there are two creation stories written at different times by different authors. They both contradict and complement each other. We compared the two in detail, and we were all amazed. The stories didn't even agree on what came first, human beings or vegetation!"

"Listen," said Janet, "I think God's Word is God's Word. Some scholars want to complicate things by introducing all these fancy theories about different authors and editors and whatnot. I just think we should live our lives by the Bible's simple truths. Don't you?"

"I agree that we shouldn't make things overly complicated. Our lives are complicated enough without adding unnecessarily to them."

"Amen to that!" replied Janet.

"But I actually think that I am reading the Bible a lot more plainly and simply than you are."

"How so?" asked Janet, biting her tongue.

"To me it's far more complicated to run intellectual circles around all the differences between Genesis 1 and Genesis 2 than to acknowledge that we're reading two different stories that both have something meaningful to say. If I'm not threatened by the fear that everything will fall apart over even one contradiction, then reading Genesis this way seems perfectly natural and unforced. I tried to reconcile the two stories. I really did! But my head was spinning from all the complicated and unlikely assumptions I had to make. Then I realized that even if I could hold together all these swirling assumptions, I'd still have to come up with all kinds of theories about why carbon-14 dating is incorrect and why scientists for the last two hundred years are all wrong. To me, many people's 'plain and simple' reading of the Bible is anything but plain or simple."

"I'm not sure I agree, but tell me where you think salvation stands if death is part of God's plan rather than being the result of sin."

"Actually, I don't read the story of Adam and Eve in the same way you do. I think the writer is telling a supremely good story about human growth and development that happens naturally and our response to it."

"Are you denying the reality of sin, then?"

"Not at all. In fact, I think the story of Adam and Eve tells us quite a bit about how we experience sin. Adam blames Eve for eating the fruit, Eve blames the serpent, and both were hiding from God to begin with. To me, that's the writer's way of showing us that sin alienates us from God, each other, and the rest of God's Creation."

"So you think death is part of God's original design—something that God felt was good from the beginning?"

"When I read other passages from the Bible, I find lots of affirmation about the goodness of God's Creation. And I mean God's present Creation, not the one before the supposed Fall. In some places, like the Book of Job, even the scarier and deadlier qualities of certain animals are praised for revealing God's glory. Jesus himself talked about finding God in Creation. When I look around me, I just don't see that the presence of death challenges God's goodness. If there wasn't death, our whole ecosystem would break down. Without death, God's blessing to "be fruitful and multiply" would become a curse. Bringing life into the world would overrun the whole planet."

"But if God approves of death," Janet pressed, "how is Christ our Savior?"

"I think there's real evil in the world, but evil isn't what causes death and pain. Evil may use death and pain—and anything else, including love—as instruments. Jesus reveals a God who became flesh, suffered, and died for the life of God's Creation. When I look at the world, I see that death and resurrection are built into the very order of things. Jesus reveals that death and resurrection are part of God's goodwill and intent from the beginning. Part of the reason I consider Jesus my Savior is because he shows me that I can trust the basic pattern rather than fight against it. And not just in a physical sense."

"What do you mean?" Janet queried.

"You know my life. There have been some incredibly painful periods. When things have gotten crazy, I've turned to Jesus with faith, trusting that all things can be made new. Life can be raised out of the worst of situations."

Janet and Linda continued to converse about Creation, Jesus, and other topics of faith for another hour or so. Before they parted, they expressed appreciation to each other. Neither one walked away from the coffeehouse converted to the other's views. In fact, Janet still believes strongly in a literal six-day Creation (and not intelligent design). While she feels that creationism should be taught in Kansas science courses, she's less threatened than before by arguments that it should not. She now sees that those who have another view are not all seeking to dismantle the Christian faith but may be sincere believers. She assured Linda that she would never again speak of "people of faith" as if the designation applied only to creationists. On the other hand, while Linda continues to feel teaching the biblical Creation stories should not be part of the science curriculum, she now feels they should be taught in certain classes dealing with the literature of Western civilization. She also realizes that if the debates between Creation and evolution are to ever have hope of moving beyond their current dysfunctionality, the focus must shift from basic science to basic theology.

WALKING THE TALK

The conversation between Janet and Linda models, in part, what can happen when Christians take Affirmations 8 and 10 seriously. Both women took the time—and had the incentive—to listen to one another rather than merely debate. Both asserted strong points of view while simultaneously looking for the other's "right answers." They both tried to find a new "right answer" that might transcend their points of view. In the process of conversation, they each saw the other's beliefs in a different framework. Rather than being converted to the other's views, they each left having moved somewhat toward one another without sacrificing their own beliefs. If they were to continue to discuss creationism and science with others in a similar vein and those conversations were added to a myriad of other similar ones, it is possible that a new kind of bridge could emerge between opposing viewpoints, one that looks nothing like what any of the sides might see right now.

I believe that one of the lasting achievements of such continual, broad-based, and respectful discussions might be that eventually, when people hear the words *Christian* and *Creation* used in the same sentence, they will not immediately think of people arguing over evidence for or against the existence of God or salvation. Rather they will envision people caught up in the awe and wonder of Creation, who view science not as an enemy but as an enabler in the attempt to give adequate praise to their God.

eleven

**Caring for our bodies and insisting on taking time
to enjoy the benefits of prayer, reflection, worship,
and recreation in addition to work**

AS CHRISTIANS, WE STRIVE to embrace and embody ways of living that promote the health of the body, the joy of living, and the benefits attained when work is combined with rest and recreation, reflection and prayer. We do this for our sake, for the sake of others, for the sake of the earth, and for the sake of Christ.

WE AFFIRM that the Path of Jesus is found where Christ's followers care for their bodies as temples of the holy and take time to pray and play, to worship, and to reflect, as essential parts of their vocation.

WE CONFESS that we have moved away from this Path when we have supported the ethics of Pharaoh over the ethics of God by promoting systems of production and consumption without attending to the disciplines of rest and recreation, reflection and prayer. We have further moved from the Path when we have denigrated or abused our bodies or those of others or denied the rights and responsibilities of others to make decisions about how they care for the bodies God gave them.

*The feeling of being hurried is not usually the result of living a full
life and having no time. It is on the contrary born of a vague
fear that we are wasting our life. When we do not do the
one thing we ought to do, we have no time for anything
else—we are the busiest people in the world.*

—ERIC HOFFER, *Reflections on the Human Condition*

A country pastor is out fishing on his day off. A parishioner spots him and says, "You know, Pastor, the Devil doesn't take a day off."

"And if I didn't take a day off," replies the pastor, "I'd be just like him!"

Can you relate? This story seems to represent our cultural attitudes a little too closely. Americans work harder and longer than any other workers in industrialized countries—on average, 49½ weeks a year, which is 6½ more weeks a year than British workers, 3½ more weeks even than Japanese workers, and 12½ more weeks than German workers. We have an average of thirteen paid vacation days per year, the lowest number among workers in Japan, Korea, Brazil, and most of Europe. A third of us eat lunch and work at the same time and never leave the building once we get there.

I once visited a megachurch in Orange County, California, to pay a visit to a couple of associate ministers I'd met on a trip to Turkey the year before. At the time, the church was pushing the theme of "finding more margin in your life," meaning making rest, prayer, and recreation a priority. The ministers were complaining bitterly about their work environment. "Every time we try to practice what we're preaching, we get hounded by the senior ministers for not being committed enough to our work!"

The deadly sin of sloth runs deep in America. Yes, sloth! When I was researching my last book, dealing with the Seven Deadly Sins, I assumed that sloth is one of the least problematic sins for Americans.[1] After all, aren't we working harder than any other industrialized nation? Yet I discovered that the sloth, in its true meaning, is one of our most serious problems. It has nothing to do with laziness *per se*. According to the ancients, sloth can have as much to do with busyness as idleness. In our society, the most slothful among us are often the ones putting in the most hours at work.

We find this peculiar notion underlying the apostle Paul's words in 2 Thessalonians 3:6–13. Here he accuses some members of the congregation of "living in idleness." They don't do "any work." So far, it sounds like they fit our modern definition of sloth. But in his next breath, Paul also calls these people "busybodies." How can one be both a busybody and slothful?

The Greek word that the New Revised Standard Version of the Bible renders *busybody* actually means "to bustle about uselessly," "to be preoccupied with trifling matters." It also means "to take more pains about a thing that it warrants," "to waste one's labor." In other words, Paul understands slothful behavior as more than a failure to do anything. It's failure to do anything *that matters*. Sloth, or *acedia*, as Thomas Aquinas called it, has to do with "not caring" (which is what *acedia* literally means). While not caring about unimportant matters is a blessing ("Don't sweat the small stuff," we say), not caring about what does matter is a big problem. We live in a society convinced that if we just run on a hamster wheel long and hard enough, someone will let us off someday and we can enjoy a life of rest and leisure. Though we're smart enough to know we can't enjoy the "good life" without hard work, we're shortsighted enough to believe that sacrificing rest and leisure throughout most of our lives in order to have it later on makes sense.

Jesus once told a story about a hardworking rich man who produced abundantly. The man thought to himself, "What should I do, for I have no place to store my crops?" Then he said, "I will do this: I will pull down my barns and build larger ones, and there I will store all my grain and my goods. And I will say to my soul, 'Soul, you have ample goods laid up for many years; relax, eat, drink, be merry.'" But then God says to him, "You fool! This very night, your life is being demanded of you. And the things you have prepared, whose will they be?" Jesus concluded his story with the observation, "So it is with those who store up treasures for themselves but are not rich toward God." To Jesus, being "rich toward God" means taking the time to do what matters for the soul throughout our lives, not just at the end of life. If we get used to sacrificing what matters in the name of enjoying the "good life" in the end, we rarely receive what we bargained for. By the time we retire, we're either so used to the hamster wheel that we continue running on it (how often have you heard the comment, "I need to retire from my retirement"?), or we simply poop out altogether, doing little more than watching television and perhaps playing golf.[2]

In his book *Fire in the Belly*, Sam Keen reflects on an encounter with Howard Thurman at Harvard University, who had a way of getting down to issues that matter to the soul:

That first day of seminar . . . , [Thurman] sat on the edge of the table for an eternity or so, not saying a word, looking at the dozen members of the class—I mean *really* looking. Finally, in a slow rich voice, he began to read from Admiral Byrd's account of being alone and near death at the North Pole. When he finished, he paused and asked, "If you were alone, a thousand miles from any other person, it was fifty degrees below zero, and you were dying, what would have to have happened to allow you to die with integrity and a sense of completion?" The question dropped down beneath all the manufactured certainties of my mind and exploded in my gut like a depth charge. I knew I was in the presence of a man who thought with his mind, heart, and body stretched to their fullest.[3]

One of the things I like best about the first Creation story in the Book of Genesis (1:1–2:4a) is that it reveals an understanding of life that, if taken seriously, helps us align our busy lives with what matters. The first thing to note is that according to the Hebrew conception (still true today in Jewish Sabbath practice), day actually begins with night: "And there was evening and there was morning, the first day." This concept of "day" thoroughly subverts our sense of self-importance. When we rise in the morning thinking that the day has just begun, it's actually half over according to Genesis. While we've been sleeping, God's Creation has been getting by just fine without us. Yet so often we spring out of bed in the morning half believing that the world has been at a complete standstill waiting with bated breath until we rise so it can function properly again. As Eugene Peterson notes in his book *Working the Angles*, perhaps instead of launching into our plans for the day, we should seek each morning to discern what God has already been up to and ask God how we may join in with those plans.[4]

When we adapt our lives to the patterns of watching and reflecting before doing and achieving, we ultimately waste a lot less time spinning our wheels. We chase after empty dreams and neglect what matters to the soul. Far better to "sweat the big stuff" so that we don't waste time and energy on the small stuff.

Another thing I find intriguing about the Creation story is what happens on the seventh day. God rests. We're not told why God had to rest, just that God rested. If God finds it necessary to rest and be refreshed, what makes us so sure we can live a creative life without doing the same? This point is brought home in the Book of Exodus on three separate occasions, one of them smack in the heart of the Ten Commandments. Here God not only gives the command to rest on the seventh day but justifies it by pointing back to the Creation of heaven and earth: "For in six days the LORD made heaven and earth, the sea, and all that is in them, but rested the seventh day; therefore the LORD blessed the Sabbath day and consecrated it" (Exodus 20:8–11).

In the Book of Deuteronomy, this same Sabbath command is repeated as part of the Ten Commandments, only its justification is different: "Remember that you were a slave in the land of Egypt, and the LORD your God brought you out from there with a mighty hand and an outstretched arm; therefore the LORD your God commanded you to keep the Sabbath day (Deuteronomy 5:15).

In other words, not only are rest and relaxation necessary for staying creative, but without them, we're little more than slaves in this world. It doesn't matter how wealthy we are; we might as well be back in Egypt working under Pharaoh. The most important event in the entire Old Testament is God's liberation of the Hebrew slaves from bondage to Pharaoh. Linking the Sabbath command to this liberation event effectively says, "If you don't integrate at least one full day of deep rest into your life, not even God can liberate you!" And because the Hebrews are commanded to grant time off not only to themselves but also to everyone in their household, their livestock, their own slaves, and immigrants residing among them, the implication is that giving rest is not only a matter of liberation but one of basic justice. Within this ancient and very different historical context, the point about rest becomes even more pronounced: the Hebrews are to grant rest even to those who theoretically have no right to it by virtue of status.

I believe that future generations will look back at our time and wonder why we did not see more clearly that one of the biggest issues of social justice in our day was the need to give ourselves and others more opportunity for rest. We are so used to running the hamster wheel at breakneck speed that we hardly have time to notice that rest is not a luxury. Our children, if they are fortunate, will be wiser.

WALKING THE TALK

Some people will no doubt interpret this affirmation to imply the need to return to the days of blue laws in America, when failure to rest on the (Christian) Sabbath was punishable by law. This always worked better in theory than in practice. The fact that different religions recognize different days as their Sabbath should be enough reason to warrant caution. And even in Jesus' day, when a single day (Saturday) was commonly recognized among Jews for Sabbath observance, Jesus continually reminded people to see beyond its legal requirement to the heart of what it was all about: "The Sabbath was made for humankind, and not humankind for the Sabbath" (Mark 2:27). When the Pharisees challenged Jesus for healing on the Sabbath, Jesus countered, "Is it lawful to do good or to do harm on the Sabbath, to save life or to kill?" (Mark 3:4).

Still, it must be recognized that Christians have more often than not taken Jesus' challenges to the Sabbath as license for ignoring it altogether—a fact that surely would have struck Jesus as far worse than the abuses he was protesting to begin with.

There is a Chinese expression that goes, "It is hard to see the dragon that has swallowed you." The depth to which our culture is absorbed in busyness currently suggests that one of the biggest implications of Affirmation 11 is that we need to start talking to one another about what Sabbath means in our day and age and what the integration of rest and relaxation, prayer and play and worship in everyday life really looks like on a personal and communal level. What does Sabbath look like in other cultures where people in the modern world have realized greater success than we have? Should we, for instance, move to a thirty-five-hour workweek, as the French have done in the past, or insist on more vacation time? What would be the implications of doing so? What would we give up and what would we gain as a society? Would such measures serve the cause of justice or hinder it?

Until we work these issues out as a nation, it seems equally clear that there are things we can be doing right now as communities of faith and as individuals to begin practicing what we preach. As individuals, we can insist on living by the standards of Affirmation 11 as a matter of personal choice. We can evaluate our personal priorities, asking ourselves Howard Thurman's question, "What would have to have happened [in your life] to allow you to die with integrity and a sense of completion?"

Perhaps the largest implication of Affirmation 11 is that there is hope. Life really is more than work. Life really can become creative, liberating, and justice-oriented again. But we have to reevaluate our priorities and then live by them.

There is a story about a business consultant who met with a group of busy young executives to teach time management skills. The consultant began, "No doubt you have heard the expression, 'I'm having the time of my life.' But time *is* life. It's what we live in. And *this* is your life." The consultant pointed to a large empty vase on the table. "This vase represents your time, your priorities, what you do with your life." Next, the consultant put three large stones in the vase until they reached its mouth and asked the executives if it was full. They said it was.

"Wrong!" the consultant countered, producing a bag of gravel from under the table and pouring its contents into the jar until gravel reached its mouth. Then he asked again if the jar was full. "Yes," the executives said.

"Wrong!" The clever consultant produced another bag, this one full of sand, dumping it on top of the gravel and stones. "*Now* is it full?"

Less quick to answer this time, a couple of the executives finally ventured, "No?"

"Correct!" answered the consultant, producing a flask of water and pouring it over the sand, gravel, and stones. "Now. Is. It. Full?"

"Uh . . . yes?" one meekly hazarded.

"Correct! Now, who can tell me why we just did this?"

One particularly eager young executive exclaimed, "To teach us that no matter how busy we think we are, we can always squeeze a little more into our schedule!"

"Wrong!" answered the consultant. "This exercise demonstrates that unless you put the big things in first, you'll never get them in at all."

twelve

**Acting on the faith that we are born with a meaning
and purpose, a vocation and ministry that serve to
strengthen and extend God's realm of love**

As Christians, we practice prayer as a daily discipline, seeking both to enjoy God's presence and to discern God's will for our lives and our faith communities. We accept it as one of our highest responsibilities and privileges to help those in our communities of faith discern God's direction for their lives and to celebrate and value their discernment in the worship and missional life of the church. In every available way, we seek to help people develop and use their diverse callings as an expression of their faith.

We affirm that the Path of Jesus is found where all of Christ's followers are understood to be called into a ministry. God's intention for us can be found and followed, however haltingly and imperfectly, in obedience to the guidance and insights, which come in prayer. We hold this conviction to be true of the church as well as of each of its members.

We confess that we have moved away from this Path when we have claimed that one form of ministry is any higher or more sacred than any other, inside or outside a church. Further, we have moved from the Path when we have failed to concretely value meaningful input and participation by both laypeople and clergy in the worship and mission of our communities.

The commitments of the Christian life are not about something
we have to do to get saved. *They are about what we do to move*
our lives into the passion and excitement and joy of
the Christian drama: the Christian Way.

— BRUCE VAN BLAIR

"Are you *saved*?" We hear this question frequently from certain Christians. To some, salvation has to do with a single point or moment of decision in one's life that determines one's eternal fate.

This has always struck me as odd, given, as we observed in Affirmation 9, that the biblical notion of salvation has overwhelmingly to do with what happens here on earth and is only secondarily concerned with otherworldly matters. My friend Bruce Van Blair says it well: "The question that goes with conversion is not 'Are you saved?' The question that goes with conversion is 'Are you used?'"

To the early Christians, being "saved" meant that you converted from living for yourself to living for God. This put you in a new path or way of life (Christianity was originally called simply "The Way"). On this path, you found your true identity and purpose, one that had been a part of you since the beginning of life but never really grew or blossomed until God became its end point.

The New Testament letter to the Ephesians says, "For by grace you have been saved through faith, and this is not your own doing; it is the gift of God, not the result of works." Then in the very next breath the author concludes, "For we are what

[God] has made us, created in Christ Jesus for good works, which God prepared beforehand to be our Way of life" (Ephesians 2:8–9).

In other words, whether it be the result of a sudden awakening or a gradual one, at some point we stop hitting the snooze button in life and wake up to discover that just as surely as the sun has been shining gently on our face before we awakened, so surely has a wild and untamable Love surrounded us from the very beginning. And it will be our end.

When we finally awaken to this literal "amazing grace," we begin losing interest in anything that distracts us from the awe and wonder of this awareness. Thus some areas of our lives that used to be considered important are dropped like so much dead weight. Other areas, however, gain a new meaning and significance as we finally discover why something deep within lit up whenever we wandered into their territory. "Aha!" we say. "This is why I've always loved doing it so much!"

When the author of Ephesians notes that we are "created in Christ Jesus for good works," he isn't talking about merely serving on church committees. He's talking about devoting ourselves to doing whatever it is that brings us fully alive in this world and gives our souls rest. This is why we're here to begin with. This is what our truest self really wants to be doing.

Many Christians consider discipleship to be little more than a hobby—a serious one, but a hobby nonetheless. Christianity is not a hobby. It is a vocation. A calling. Accompanying each and every conversion that has ever happened on the face of the earth, whether sudden or gradual, is a calling to full-time service to

God. According to the ancient tradition, if one is not serving God full time, one has not truly been converted. There is no such thing as a part-time Christian. This means a critical part of our path in life is discerning what God is calling us to do.

Most of us are all too happy to leave God out of the equation. We're accustomed to being made to feel guilty by well-meaning church people who want us to do or not do certain things. We suspect that if we truly perceived a calling from God it would be to join a monastery or work on the streets of Calcutta like Mother Teresa. To be sure, some people are called to such vocations. When they sense the call, they feel bliss, not guilt. The vast majority of us are not called to these vocations. Whatever it is we are truly called to do resonates with deep chords inside us that have likely excited us for as long as we can remember. When God strums those chords, we feel joy, not guilt. So unless you consistently feel joy when considering becoming a monk or Mother Teresa, their path is probably not yours.

Saint Teresa of Avila once advised, "Do whatever arouses you most to love." This is what God wants of us. The Hebrew scriptures affirm that we are created in the very image and likeness of God. Why trust someone else's conception of what you should be "doing for God" if it doesn't light up and bring joy to that piece of your soul that God created? God isn't such an imbecile as to call you into doing something that has nothing to do with what brings you alive in this world. It may not fit into "churchy" categories, but that's the church's problem, not yours.

Where I grew up, on Mercer Island, Washington, there was a service station owned by devout Muslims who had a great reputation for fixing cars. You knew that whatever was ailing your automobile would be fixed correctly, at a fair price, with impeccable honesty. You could trust that they'd never fix anything that didn't need fixing. When asked about their motivation for working so hard and being so honest, they would reply that they were called by Allah into their profession. To them, this meant that they needed to fix cars as if Muhammad himself were riding in them.

These mechanics demonstrate the beauty of what happens when people discover what brings them alive in this world and use it to serve God. The mechanics had not the slightest sense that theirs was a profession any lower than that of a prophet, priest, or king.

In the Christian tradition, the apostle Paul articulates this same understanding when he says, "*Whatever* your task, work heartily, as serving the Lord and not men, knowing that from the Lord you will receive the inheritance as your reward; *you are serving the Lord Christ*" (Colossians 3:23–24).

What part of "whatever" don't Christians understand? One of the truly remarkable things about following an authentic sense of call is that it leads us straight to the heart of our bliss, whether what we are doing falls into traditionally religious categories or not. In this regard, God seems content to stir the deepest waters of our soul even if we have no idea it is God doing it or if we don't interpret what's going on in Christian terms.

In a 2004 interview with Neil Young on her National Public Radio show *Fresh Air*, host Terri Gross asked him about his evolving playing style and what influenced him. Young's response articulated well what it is like to seek that place inside us where God is stirring the soul. He said that guitar playing is like "deep-earth mining." He just keeps banging away and blasting through in an effort to get to the core. He said, "Every solo I am looking for a way to go deeper. I'm looking for how am I going to lose myself. How can I get to a point where nothing matters? How can I stop thinking? How can I lose track of what's going on and still be in sync?"

When Gross asked Young about the origins of his distinctive sound, Young told her that he had found it instinctively, when he was about seventeen. He and his band and some other musicians were playing a song by the Premiers called "Farmer John." He got so into his guitar solo that he "just kept going and going and grinding and just pounding away at this rhythmic thing and exploring little nuances of it." When he came off stage, one of the much more experienced guitarists asked him how he could do what Young had just done. At first, Young just said that he was doing what he had always been doing, but the other musician told him it wasn't even close. He told Young he had no idea how Young had played the way he did. Young said, "At that point, I realized that there's a place I can go. I just kind of fell into it by accident. And I think I've spent the rest of my life trying to get there."

Neil Young may not articulate his sense of call in traditionally religious terms, but his sense of how that call is perceived and what it feels like to surrender to it is very much in keeping with traditional religious understandings. He may not claim to be "serving the Lord, not men," to use Paul's language, but he clearly understands his vocation as seeking the transcendent voice beckoning from deep within him and surrendering to it. That's the purpose of life. That's where life is to be oriented. Who can say that Neil Young does not serve the world or Christ when he does this? Christ does not belong to the church. The church belongs to Christ. God is not confined to our conceptions. (See Affirmation 3 in this regard.)

To affirm that people can be following God's calling completely apart from their religious affiliation or understanding of God does not in any way diminish the value of being Christian and realizing the Source of one's call. If anything, it increases it. As in other great faith traditions of the world, Christians have discovered over thousands of years a way of articulating what's going on in the soul, and how God whispers to it, with a high degree of precision (as much precision as one can have in these matters, anyway). I'm not talking about the Christian televangelists or those who claim that all that matters in life is to accept Jesus as Lord and go to Heaven. Rather, I'm talking about the Christian mystics, the great theologians and preachers over the centuries and others in modern times who see below the surface. These people have found a way of describing what's going on using language and thought forms particular to our tradition. Those familiar with the tradition can link up literally throughout the ages with others who have had similar experiences and learn from each of them. It's like a great body of medical knowledge in which surgeons can go back hundreds and thousands of years to refine their skills by learning from the practices of others. It's a truly magnificent thing to be a Christian attuned to

Christian spirituality because it puts you in touch with wisdom that can help you track and follow your bliss more consistently, deeply, and joyously.

However, just as the healing arts are not ultimately dependent on medical ways of describing them, so salvation and God's calling are not dependent on Christian—or Buddhist or Hindu or Taoist or Muslim—ways of describing them. Does this mean that Christianity is not important in the spiritual quest? The answer is found in how you would answer a surgeon if, after discovering that it's possible to heal people in nonsurgical ways, she asks if she should abandon her craft as unimportant. Would you tell her, "Yes, all is lost"? Or would you say, "This is the path God has given you to practice. It is a good, righteous, and healing path. Don't throw it away. Rather, delve all the more deeply into it, even as you acknowledge other forms of healing arts as appropriate. By following your particular path, many will be saved"?

WALKING THE TALK

If you are still concerned that the examples I've used aren't Christian enough, let us turn to Christendom itself and consider something that should be of even greater concern to Christians. Every Sunday in church pews across America—in the very place where people's perception of God's call and response to it should be of utmost concern—millions of Christians sit with no idea of what to do with the experiences they've had that bring them alive in this world. They have no idea because unless their souls' stirrings are inspiring them to serve on a committee or become a youth leader or give more generously or participate in a mission project, their church couldn't care less about what they're feeling. In fact, it is easy to get the impression that as long as one spends two or three hours a week volunteering, even God couldn't care less about the forty or more hours one spends at work.

This is not, of course, the case in all churches. Yet ask yourself, "How many times have I heard my minister preach about how car mechanics or rock musicians can serve Jesus with just as much integrity as the Mother Teresas of the world? And if you do hear such affirmations, how many times do you actually hear from the mechanics and musicians in the pulpit? Are those who put their Christianity into practice in these ways held high as models for the rest of us? Is their advice sought about spiritual discernment and the practice of ministry?"

Happily, in the emerging church, this very thing is happening. Bit by bit across the country, a new understanding of the Reformation principle of the Priesthood of All Believers is taking shape, one which takes this principle more seriously than even the great reformers did. Consequently, laypeople in secular professions *are* being held up as models. Their input *is* actively sought in planning and leading worship and mission. However, this movement appears to be not much more than the growing edge of Christianity. It is far from the norm.

Of course, many members of our society are not working in professions that bring them alive in this world. Their job is just a paycheck and nothing more. Yet is this not all the more reason why churches should spend time focusing on discerning and following what brings their members alive in this world?

Affirmation 12 means that the church should care—a lot—about helping people find their sense of purpose, their sense of adventurousness and vitality, their sense of awe and wonder and joy in their vocations. The church should be the first place, not the last, where people who have discerned a sense of call and followed it are held high and celebrated, serving as models for others. If it does not, then making money and conspicuous consumption will continue to be the number one goal and pastime in American culture. After all, why wouldn't it be if, even in churches, no one cares about finding fulfillment and purpose in one's vocation?

NOTES

Introduction

1 *Newsweek*/Beliefnet Poll, "Where We Stand on Faith," *Newsweek* (August 29, 2005, pp. 48–49). The complete poll results may be found at http://www.beliefnet.com/story/173/story_17353_1.html.

2 Assuming that three (rather than two) of the nearly nine people who identify themselves as Christian go to church, this means that seven of every ten do not go to church. Assuming that a third of those who attend church have significant reservations, this means that eight in every ten Christians in America either are frustrated with their faith community or have dropped out entirely.

3 This notion is commonly attributed to Teilhard de Chardin, although others, from Wayne Dyer to Ram Das, also speak in these terms.

4 Marcus Borg, *The Heart of Christianity* (San Francisco: HarperSanFrancisco, 2004), p. xii.

5 The original clergy group is called No Longer Silent: Clergy for Justice, which has gathered in the Phoenix area since 1997.

6 See Matthew 22:34–40, Mark 12:28–31, and Luke 10:25–28; compare these to Deuteronomy 6:5 and Leviticus 19:18.

Affirmation 2

1 Of course, some people will argue that the latter command negates the former one because the former command is from the Old Testament whereas the latter is from the New Testament. This line of reasoning has always struck me as odd. How can you insist that the entire Bible is literally true and without error and in the next breath claim that three-quarters of the Bible is obsolete?

2 Michael Burlingame (ed.), *Lincoln Observed: The Civil War Dispatches of Noah Brooks* (Baltimore: Johns Hopkins University Press, 1998), p. 210.

Affirmation 3

1 There is in fact a whole body of literature commonly referred to as Wisdom Literature that looks to nature as a primary revealer of God's glory

and wisdom. The books of Proverbs, Ecclesiastes, and Job are representative. For an example of God's very Self being revealed in the natural order, read Job 38:1–42:6. Here God speaks to Job "out of a whirlwind," answering a series of complaints Job has lodged against God. After four full chapters of God's description of the natural world, Job is thoroughly humbled and declares, "I have heard you with the hearing of the ear, but now my eye sees you."

Affirmation 4

1 Leon Wieseltier, *Congregation: Contemporary Writers Read the Jewish Bible* (Orlando, Fla.: Harcourt Brace, 1989), p. 33.

Affirmation 5

1 William Sloane Coffin, *Credo* (Louisville, Ky.: Westminster/John Knox, 2004), p. 138.

2 To "change one's way of thinking" is actually the literal meaning of the Greek word *metanoia*, which is normally translated in the Bible as "repent."

3 Larry Rasmussen, "Are We Missing Another Chance to Be Lutheran?" *The Lutheran*, July 2005, p. 29. *Justification* is a theological term denoting the "setting right in the eyes of God." Luther claimed that all people, no matter what their background, may be set right in the eyes of God by grace acting through faith in Jesus Christ. In other words, we are saved by faith, not by works of righteousness. Salvation has more to do with God's goodness than with our goodness.

4 Antoinette Brown Blackwell became the first ordained woman in America in 1853. She graduated from Oberlin College and carried on a Christian ministry for some time before being officially recognized through ordination. She was active in the women's movement throughout her life, sharing a number of public platforms with Susan B. Anthony and Julia Ward Howe.

5 There are no more than six passages in all of Scripture that could be construed as dealing with what we call homosexuality (the topic itself is never mentioned in the Bible, as there was no term for it in Greek, Hebrew, or Aramaic). Compare this with the more than two thousand passages in the Bible that deal with wealth, use of material possessions, and our responsibility toward the poor, and one gets the idea pretty fast

where Scripture focuses its attention with respect to life in community with others.

Affirmation 6

1 David U. Himmelstein, Elizabeth Warren, Deborah Thorne, and Steffie Woolhandler, "Illness and Injury as Contributors to Bankruptcy," *Health Affairs*, February 2, 2005, pp. 63–73.

Affirmation 7

1 James Madison, "A Memorial and Remonstrance," address to the General Assembly of the Commonwealth of Virginia (1785), cited in George Seldes (ed.), *The Great Quotations* (Secaucus, N.J.: Citadel Press), pp. 459–460.

2 D. James Kennedy, in materials handed out to participants at a national conference sponsored by the Center for Reclaiming America, February 18–19, 2005, Coral Ridge Presbyterian Church. Reported in Jane Lampman, "For Evangelicals, a Bid to 'Reclaim America,'" *Christian Science Monitor*, March 16, 2005.

3 See 2 Samuel 12:1–12, where Nathan calls David to account for committing adultery with Bathsheba.

Affirmation 8

1 "It is almost certain that this is a wind of torment and evil that Allah has sent to this American empire," a Kuwaiti official wrote in the Arabic daily *Al-Siyassa* under the headline "The Terrorist Katrina Is One of the Soldiers of Allah."

2 "In my belief, God judged New Orleans for the sin of shedding innocent blood through abortion," said Steve Lefemine, who e-mailed the flesh-toned weather map to fellow activists across the country and put a stark message on the answering machine of his organization, Columbia Christians for Life. "Providence punishes national sins by national calamities," it said. "Greater divine judgment is coming upon America unless we repent of the national sin of abortion." (Lefemine was quoted in Alan Cooperman, "Where Most See a Weather System, Some See Divine Retribution," *Washington Post*, September 4, 2005, p. A27.)

3 "Katrina Disaster? Just Blame Bush" was the title of an article by Charles Cutter, who wrote, "George W. Bush did not cause the destruction of

New Orleans, just as he did not cause the 9/11 attacks. In both cases, however, he had ample warnings that he ignored. . . . Like Hurricane Katrina, George W. Bush has been a foreseeable disaster" (*Magic City Morning Star*, Millinocket, Maine, September 2, 2005).

4   Some of the extremist right-wing punditry following the hurricane centered around hurricane victims having been beholden to a perceived welfare mentality promulgated by Democrats, which was claimed to have led them to trust the government rather than their own ingenuity and resources to deal with disaster.

5   "We take no joy in the death of innocent people," commented Michael Marcavage of Repent America, an organization calling for "a nation in rebellion toward God" to reclaim its senses. "But we believe that God is in control of the weather. . . . The day Bourbon Street and the French Quarter was flooded was the day that 125,000 homosexuals were going to be celebrating sin in the streets [as part of the Southern Decadence Festival]. . . . We're calling it an act of God." Interestingly enough, Bourbon Street and the French Quarter were about the only places in New Orleans that were left high and dry. (Marcavage was quoted in Cooperman, "Where Most See a Weather System," p. A27.)

6   "Is this some sort of bizarre coincidence? Not for those who believe in the God of the Bible." So wrote a Christian journalist for the Web site Jerusalem Newswire, who saw it as more than a coincidence that at the same time people were being evacuated from their homes in New Orleans, Jewish settlers were being removed from their homes in the Gaza Strip. (Stan Goodenough, "Katrina: The Fist of God?" Jerusalem Newswire, August 29, 2005; http://www.jnewswire.com.)

7   Christine Byl, "Language of Devotion: A Conversation with David James Duncan," (*Sun*, 276: December 1998, p. 9.)

Affirmation 9

1   Throughout the centuries, Christians have found in Jesus' simple prayer of forgiveness for those who are crucifying him a sign that God's love and grace extend to all people, the righteous and the unrighteous alike.

2   Many people quote only the first sentence (verse 16) in making a case that God intends to save only those who believe in Jesus and condemn

those who do not. However, the second sentence (verse 17) counters these assumptions. God's intention is to save the world. Although some Christians may assert that there is a difference between what God intends and what God gets, one of the consistent signs of God's power in Scripture is that God eventually gets everything God intends, no matter how long it takes and no matter how it may confound human imagination—particularly with respect to salvation. See, for instance, Isaiah 55:1–11, and compare Isaiah 45:22–23 and Romans 11:26–36.

Affirmation 11

1 Eric Elnes, *Igniting Worship: The Seven Deadly Sins* (Nashville, Tenn.: Abingdon, 2004). See also my segment on sloth at the movies in "Faith and Film," in *Cloud of Witnesses*, an audio journal published by Princeton Theological Seminary's Institute for Youth Ministry (http://www.ptsem.edu/iym).

2 Before you write me a letter, let me make it perfectly clear that I have nothing against golf! I hope to play when I retire myself. I am simply saying that a life full of nothing but golf, or golf and television, is not really what the spiritual life is meant to give us.

3 Sam Keen, *Fire in the Belly: On Being a Man* (New York: Bantam, 1991), p. 158.

4 Eugene H. Peterson, *Working the Angles: The Shape of Pastoral Integrity* (Grand Rapids, Mich.: Eerdmans, 1987).

THE PHOENIX AFFIRMATIONS

1 Walking fully in the Path of Jesus without denying the legitimacy of other paths that God may provide for humanity

2 Listening for God's Word, which comes through daily prayer and meditation, studying the ancient testimonies which we call Scripture, and attending to God's present activity in the world

3 Celebrating the God whose Spirit pervades and whose glory is reflected in all of God's Creation, including the earth and its ecosystems, the sacred and secular, the Christian and non-Christian, the human and non-human

4 Expressing our love in worship that is as sincere, vibrant, and artful as it is scriptural

5 Engaging people authentically, as Jesus did, treating all as creations made in God's very image, regardless of race, gender, sexual orientation, age, physical or mental ability, nationality, or economic class

6 Standing, as Jesus does, with the outcast and oppressed, the denigrated and afflicted, seeking peace and justice with or without the support of others

7 Preserving religious freedom and the church's ability to speak prophetically to government by resisting the commingling of church and state

8 Walking humbly with God, acknowledging our own shortcomings while honestly seeking to understand and call forth the best in others, including those who consider us their enemies

9 Basing our lives on the faith that in Christ all things are made new and that we, and all people, are loved beyond our wildest imagination—for eternity

10 Claiming the sacredness of both our minds and our hearts, and recognizing that faith and science, doubt and belief serve the pursuit of truth

11 Caring for our bodies and insisting on taking time to enjoy the benefits of prayer, reflection, worship, and recreation in addition to work

12 Acting on the faith that we are born with a meaning and purpose, a vocation and ministry that serve to strengthen and extend God's realm of love

CPSIA information can be obtained
at www.ICGtesting.com
Printed in the USA
BVOW00n0951261216
471389BV00002BA/2/P